OPPOSITIONAL DEFIANT DISORDER

There Are no Impossible Children - Methods and Strategies to Help Parents of the Most Oppositional Kids

By:

WALTER DOUGLAS

Table of Contents

INTRODUCTION

There are no impossible children.

Dealing with a child who is often anger, irritability and provocative behavior, can seem like an endless nightmare for parents, but it is not.

Creating communication with your child is not only possible, but it is the solution to the problem.

Oppositional defiant disorder (ODD) is a negative, aggressive, and stubborn activity pattern with a period of at least six months. Negative conduct involves short-tempered behaviour, frequently arguing with adults, intentionally defying or failing to comply with the wishes or laws of adults, frequently purposely irritating others, sometimes blaming others for their own actions or misbehaviour, is sometimes touchy or easily irritated by others, is often angry and resentful, and is often despiteful or vindictive. The causes of ODD are not yet known but there are two major theories that explain a child's development of Oppositional defiant disorder.

Developmental experts believe that Strange begins at the stage of a child's infancy.

A child suffering from Oppositional defiant disorder has a greater difficulty in acquiring information as their focus is diverted by the defiance of authority particularly in school, which interferes with acquiring skills to do things independently. Another hypothesis about the causes of ODD is the passive disciplinary practices used by both professionals and parents. Taking unsolicited disciplinary actions strengthens a child's oppositional behaviour. Parents will attend parent management training focused on teaching more reliable, realistic strategies for addressing the resistance and rebellion of the child to parents of children with ODD.

Most people with Oppositional defiant disorder are kids and teenagers which include 23 per cent of kids of school age. Symptoms in children with the condition are seen as early as 2 or 3yrs in age and during pubescent years. Most kids tend to be disagreeable, disobey parents, or ignore authority when fatigued, hungry, or nervous. Kids with ODD have the same actions even though they are not exhausted, hungry or anxious, which impedes learning and the ability of a child to develop relationships with others. Some common signs include regular temper tantrums, normal protests for no apparent cause, and inability to comply with reasonable instructions and sometimes doing something contrary to what they are told to do. We are trying to get irritated with the people around them.

Kids with the condition also keep other people responsible for their acts and will most likely get into very simple discussions. We have anxiety disorders, use impolite words, pick up on other people's bad characteristics and are intentionally very rude. There are some symptoms of children with Oppositional defiant disorder and when you see there signs and symptoms in your own children, or believe your child has this disease, have a schedule with a child therapist so that they can get proper Oppositional defiant disorder treatment before it gets worse. Proper Oppositional defiant disorder diagnosis and rehabilitation often requires the use of some medications that may influence the actions of the child within a week, and it can also take a few months for the more extreme cases. Stimulant therapy is only suggested when the oppositional defiant condition coexists with the diagnosis of attention deficit / hyperactivity. No study on the use of other psychiatric drugs in the handling of oppositional defiant disorder is currently available.

What is Oppositional Defiant Disorder (ODD).

Oppositional defiant disorder is a condition with attitudes usually diagnosed during childhood. It is characterized as a continuous pattern of negativistic, defiant, disobedient, irritable, and annoying actions directed towards those in authority positions. But from time to time all kids encounter some oppositional behaviour. It only becomes an concern when their behaviour stands out as opposed to the behaviour of other children.

Children with oppositional defiant disorder are irritated quickly and deliberately annoy others. They lose their temper repeatedly; they fail to obey the rules, and blame others for their errors. We are stubborn, and continually challenge their boundaries and limits. There are also occasions when oppositional behaviour is expected in normal evolution.

Children with an oppositional defiant condition will search for and manipulate your vulnerabilities. When a parent or teacher has a bad day, they're going to pick up on it and try to make it easier. When you see mom and dad have an fight, it's when they're going to be the most trying. Dealing with these kids takes a lot of compassion, patience and understanding.

The cause of the oppositional defiant disorder is not known, but many parents report resistance problems in child development from very early on. It may have anything to do with the child's temperament, and how it responds to its disposition. A symptom-laden child should be seen by a psychiatrist or psychologist with special diagnostic training in this disorder.

To parents a child with oppositional defiant disorder can be particularly difficult. There are some ways the parents can support their kids. Praise your child for being flexible and cooperative, take some time off if you feel stressed, set boundaries and consequences, remember being consistent. Some oddly kids will react well to positive parenting.

Oppositional defiant disorder care may include certain social skills training, parental ability training, family counseling, and psychotherapy, depending on the individual needs of the individuals. Treatment varies according to age and development. The better the sooner the child is diagnosed, and the better treated.

Parental management preparation for children with oppositional defiant disorder is recommended. Parents learn to adjust their own attitudes and responses so they can help their kids do the same. Parents learn to recognise the good traits of their child and how to strengthen those behaviours.

Existing issues, such as a depressed parent, can impede successful intervention with an oppositionally defiant disordered kid. Misuse of drugs and other factors may have an extremely detrimental effect on parenting ability. For parents who are dedicated to educating themselves and developing their parenting skills, there is support available.

Signs of Oppositional Defiant Disorder?

ODD signs may include:

- Throwing repeated tantrums of rage.

- Too much conflict with adults, in particular those with authority.

- Declining to comply fully with demands and regulations.

- Trying to intentionally offend or disturb others, or becoming easily offended by others.

- Blaming your errors upon others.

- Getting regular angry and resentful outbursts.

- To be spiteful, to get revenge.

- Using obscene words or swearing.

- When angry, I say cruel and hateful things.

Additionally, many ODD children are moody, easily irritated and have poor self-esteem. Often, they may also misuse drugs and alcohol.

What Causes Oppositional Defiant Disorder?

The precise cause of ODD is unclear but it is traced back by many experts to a variety of psychological, social, and biological causes. Symptoms of ODD are frequently associated with exposure to prenatal smoke, exposure to contaminants or inadequate nutrition. ODD is more common in people with ODD, ADHD, disorder of conduct (CD), mood disorders, or substance abuse issues, although researchers have not identified a specific gene responsible. In certain people stressful life events, such as childhood violence, may cause ODD.

Often parents and teachers are the first to recognise children's oppositional actions. Then, seeing a child psychiatrist or other qualified mental health professional is the next move. To diagnose ODD accurately, a physician will conduct an evaluation to rule out anxiety or mood disorders, which can all cause behaviours similar to ODDs. Such behaviours are only Unusual "symptoms" if they occur more frequently than expected for individuals of the same age and stage of growth, and if they cause clinically significant impairment in social, academic, or occupational functioning.

An assessing physician may compile a comprehensive history of conduct from parents, teachers and clinical observation. Discussing how the action occurs with as many experts as possible and where it will help the doctor decide which habits impact various areas of the child's life. This also helps to assess how the child reacts to a challenging situation, or whether you are dealing with an ongoing behavioural problem. The physician may make a complete assessment using rating scales and questionnaires. Diagnosis is time consuming because it involves evaluation of several sources of information.

Rarely does a person with ODD take responsibility for their actions and the impact that it has on those around them. She sees lying to everyone but herself as "the problem." It typically requires a highly qualified physician to decide whether school, work or home issues trace back to Strange.

Clinicians must exclude conditions such as mood disorder (especially bipolar spectrum disorder), personality disorders (particularly unstable, trauma (physical or sexual assault), narcissistic and antisocial personality disorders), as well as drug abuse before diagnosing oppositional defiant disorder. Each of these may cause signs of ODD and oppositional behaviour.

The strain of treating ODD affects the entire family, and can strain marital relations. Luckily there are successful strategies for ruling even in the most stubborn child or adult. It's not easy to alter habits, but it can be done — usually with the aid of professional psychotherapy, a physician to supervise treatment, and medication periodically.

Some Causes of Defiant Oppositional Disorder.

The precise cause of ODD is not clear but it is suspected that a combination of genetic, biological, and environmental factors leads to the disease.

- *Biological:* Several studies indicate that abnormalities in some parts of the brain or injuries that lead to serious behavioural problems in children. ODD has also been associated with abnormal functioning of certain types of brain chemicals, or neurotransmitters. Neurotransmitters help nerve cells communicate with one another within the brain. When these hormones don't function properly, signals can not do it right in the brain, leading to ODD symptoms and other mental illnesses. In addition, many children and teens with ODD also suffer from other mental illnesses, like ADHD, depression, learning disorders, or an anxiety disorder, which can contribute to their behavioural problems.

- *Genetics:* Most adolescents and teens with ODD have near mental illness family members including mood disorders, anxiety disorders and personality disorders. This indicates a weakness may be inherited to developing Strange.

- *Environmental:* Factors such as unstable family life, family history of mental illness and/or drug abuse, and inconsistent parental discipline can contribute to behavioural disorders development.

How Is Oppositional Defiant Disorder Diagnosed?

Like with adults, children are diagnosed with mental disorders based on signs and symptoms that indicate a specific disorder such as ODD. When there are signs, the doctor will initiate an assessment by doing a full medical history and physical examination. While there are no laboratory tests for clinical diagnosis of ODD, the doctor will also use tests such as studies of neuroimaging or blood testing if they believe there may be a medical reason for the behavioural issues that arise. The doctor should also check for symptoms of other disorders frequently occurring with ODD, such as ADHD and depression.

If the doctor is unable to identify a medical reason for the symptoms, he or she will usually refer the child to a child and adolescent therapist or counselor, mental health practitioners who are specially qualified in diagnosing and treating mental illness in children and adolescents. Psychiatrists and psychologists use specially developed instruments for questioning and evaluating a child for a mental disorder. The doctor bases his/her diagnosis on observations of the child's symptoms and their evaluation of the child's actions and attitude. The doctor also needs to rely on information from the parents, teachers and other adults of the child as children often have difficulty describing their issues or recognizing their symptoms.

How to Treat Oppositional Defiant Disorder?

ODD care is calculated on the basis of several factors including the age of the child, the extent of the symptoms and the willingness of the child to engage in and accept various therapies. Treatment normally consists of a mixture of:

Psychotherapeutic

Reparation of the bond between parent and child is a priority when treating a child for ODD. That means parents have a major role to play in the care. Parent training programs are also offered to help parents learn how to improve their child's actions by setting clear goals and regularly rewarding children when they follow through and when they don't have appropriate consequences.

Parent training programs may involve work-to-work sessions with parents and children, or just parents. Other services are:

- Parent-Child Interaction Therapy (PCIT).
- Parent Management Training (PMT).
- Defiant Teens.
- Positive Parenting Program (Triple P).
- The Magnificent Years.

Many kids may also benefit from training in social skills to strengthen their peer relationships or cognitive behavioural therapy (CBT) if they struggle with anxiety or depression. Dialectical behavioural therapy (DBT) can help children dealing with severe emotional dysregulation.

Pharmacological

Unusual drug has not been authorised by FDA. However, antipsychotic medicines such as Abilify (aripiprazole) and Risperdal (risperidone) are also administered when a child is at risk of being taken away from school or home.

Stimulant medicine can be recommended if a child also has ADHD, or faces extreme impulsiveness. One antidepressant

(SSRI) can be prescribed for children with underlying depression or anxiety.

Medication

Although there is no medically proven or officially accepted treatment for treating Strange, medications may also be used to treat symptoms (impulsiveness, irritability, etc.) or other mental illnesses that may arise, such as ADHD or depression.

What Is the Outlook for Children Having Oppositional Defiant Disorder?

If your child has symptoms of Unusual it is very important to seek treatment immediately from a trained mental health professional. Without care, children with ODD can encounter rejection due to poor social skills and aggressive and irritating actions by classmates and other peers. Additionally, a child with ODD is more likely to have a more severe behavioural disorder called conduct disorder. Treatment is typically very successful when begun early.

Can Oppositional Defiant Disorder Be Prevented?

Although avoiding ODD may not be possible, identifying and acting on signs when they first occur can reduce discomfort to the child and family, and eliminate many of the problems associated with the disease. Family members may also know steps to take if there are signs of relapse (return of symptoms). Furthermore, offering a caring, welcoming and consistent home atmosphere with a combination of affection and discipline can help to alleviate symptoms and avoid rebellious behaviour episodes.

Unless you have diagnosed your child with an oppositional defiant disorder (ODD), this scenario can sound too familiar. According to the Fourth Ed. Mental Disorders Diagnostics and Statistical Manual, oppositional defiant disorder may trigger psychiatric impairment in academic, social, or occupational functioning and it's characterized by a repeated pattern of negative, rebellious, disobedient, and aggressive conduct towards authority figures that lasts for at least six months.

This is important to consider the distinctions between typical childhood attempts to resist authority and signs of full-blown oppositional defiant disorder, as children progress through several developmental stages as they grow. Nine-year-old Molly appears determined to kill adults, is persistent in her quest to prove that adults are wrong, dumb, or both, and her thoughts revolve around resisting anybody's attempt to exert control over her. Usually, she turns any encounter with adults into win / lose scenarios, and is determined to win aggressively.

Oppositional defiant children/kids share many of the following characteristics:

- They are in desperate need of influence, and they will do just about anything to obtain strength.

- Usually, they take responsibility for their crimes, and have no insight into how they influence others.

- The child with the ODD is socially exploitative and very swift to see how others react. Then he uses such responses in family or social settings, or both, to his benefit.

- These kids accept a lot of negativity–in reality they seem to thrive on large quantities of other people's tension, frustration and negativity and are always the winners in escalating battles of negativity.

Children such as Molly may also have another psychiatric disorder, in addition to oppositional defiant disorder. ODD is also a co-morbid disease of impairment of attention deficit /

hyperactivity. Tourette syndrome, anxiety and mood disorders, obsessive-compulsive disorder, Asperger's, language-processing impairments, sensory development deficiencies or even nonverbal learning difficulties may also be identified. What causes the troubling behaviour? Some researchers think many of these disorders ' symptoms may share similar neurobiological mechanisms. If one of these conditions affects your child, it's important to bear in mind that ODD will cause additional issues for you and your child.

Many parenting experts have suggested that oppositional behaviour is more common when home structure is out of balance–when there is either too much or not enough structure. The parenting is inflexible and rigid in an excessively structured setting. These "micromanage" parents come down hard on their kids and they control every part of their lives. This particular parenting style merely helps to generate greater resistance and defiance. At the other hand, excessively loose structure may also cause difficulties. Children can demonstrate oppositional defiant behaviour when parents do not provide adequate structure by setting acceptable boundaries, or by defining and monitoring consequences for misconduct. Such parents usually cede to all the demands of their kid, either out of fear of the kid or in an attempt to hold themselves in the good graces of the child. Parents should aspire to a strong and caring parenting style in which the framework is balanced in order to discourage or mitigate oppositional defiant behaviour. Parents must take responsibility and put themselves at the top of the hierarchy of the family. When parents they must use their power and at the same time make the child feel safe, cherished and soothed.

Another element to consider in avoiding oppositional behaviour, whether married or divorced, is how well the parents get along. When parents are in themselves dissatisfied or oppositional, they often disagree with parenting problems, thus greatly restricting their success in improving their child's actions. Molly is an expert at separating the authority of her parent, and would most likely benefit from manipulating rifts between her parents. Couples therapy may be in order to minimize parental tension and conflict, and set the stage for unified, effective parenting.

The significant consideration is how ODD impacts the environment. It may be one of the most traumatic situations a person faces and exacerbate stress when it is related to another medical mental illness. Family therapy will help overcome family difficulties. The family therapist will have a structured atmosphere that gives exhausted parents support and skills training.

When marital and family problems are dealt with, parents may start training both themselves and their child. Unless Molly's mother continues to respond as she always has to her quarrelsome behaviour, Molly will continue to shut her out, intensify the arguments and push the buttons of mom. Many adults engage in a disagreement about the result. During an dispute the adult's aim is to come to a resolution. In other words it is most relevant what happens as a result of the conflict. As a parent, from your viewpoint you're the one in charge because you've decided the result of the debate. The method of making an case for the oppositional child is more important to her than the result of the dispute. Nonetheless, such complaints over trivial problems that seem futile, with such a clear need for power; the goal of your child's opposition is to intensify the dispute until you are no longer in charge. That matters to her is not the topic being argued about, as much as what will happen during the debate. The opposition stubborn youth wants to decide the subject and course of the confrontation in order to influence the debate process, and seems to know instinctively when you feel most insecure and your energy is weak. At these moments, she will bring up conflict-laden topics, trying to push your buttons and distract you from problems where you are likely to seek and assert your power over her. Once your ODD kid eventually pushes your buttons she has gained control of you and the feelings in her head. She now effectively took over your place of authority at this stage. Often, when you lose control of your feelings, the level of anxiety of your child will increase along with her defensiveness. She is more oppositional as her defenses increase which is her key mechanism of defence. The problem escalates as she becomes more oppositional, and we are trapped in an endless loop of confrontation.

Conflict resolution techniques are important for de-escalating the situation. If your energy is weak, or you think the subject will give rise to an argument, it's wise to change the subject. One option to consider is to walk away from the confrontation. If you can not change the subject, or walk away it's important to note that the aim of the ODD child is to push your buttons. Think about your endurance, how long will you press the completely oppositional button? When you hit the end of your line, what choices do you have? To not take what your youngster says personally is important. When you defend yourself your child has the right to defend himself against your attack by the rules governing arguments. You get to protect yourself in response and he's now pressing your buttons and gaining strength. You don't need to justify yourself or try to reassure him you're right. Don't lower yourself to your child's oppositional point. There are two ways to stop him from pulling you in. Tell him that he has two options, in an unerruffled logical way. When he decides to stick around, he can change the subject and avoid complaining; or, when he likes, he can go somewhere in the house to complain. If your child wants to escalate, the time has come to use two strong words that can cut through any debate. Such terms ' no matter' and' notwithstanding' For example, "notwithstanding, this is how it will be..." Using such phrases repeatedly (like a broken record) will help to de-escalate the situation in a rational, unemotional way, without allowing your child to drag you into the power struggle.

It can be difficult to use effective consequences for the oppositional child, as this presents yet another opportunity for conflict in which you are likely to lose power. Discussing the repercussions when you're in the middle of their unpleasant actions would most likely cause you more anger. Therefore, concentrating on outcomes that don't require the child's participation is important. Rules and implications must be explicit, preferably in writing, to provide guidance before the dispute arises for both the child and the adult. Start by eliminating reinforcer and allowing your child to reward the products for appropriate behaviour. Reinforcer includes items such as television, stereos, CDs, video games, telephones, bicycles, skateboards, friends visiting, access to favorite clothes, favorite foods, etc. Once you've successfully avoided pushing your buttons and gaining some control over the behaviour of your child, it's time to go on the offensive to soothe her and help her get back to an even place. Oppositional children don't like getting their caretakers soothed. It takes them back to childhood role, and puts you back in the role of parent. One among the driving forces behind ODD is that a child is trying to grow up too fast for some reasons, and believes herself to be equal to her parents. Because of the amount of tension that is going on, the ODD child may feel less loved and it's hard to both feel loved as a child and try to work at an adult level. Your child may know she's loved mentally but she doesn't feel loved. Parents must be able to express love, soothe their child and nurture it. This is not always easy to accomplish, especially when past patterns of negative behaviour have become ingrained.

Non-Medical ODD Management Techniques.

The purpose of this category of strategies is to render "work" difficult for ODD. This is a way to make sure that all efforts to offend or irritate others are ineffective, and to cause war.

- ODD children are very good in putting the blame on others, including parents and/or teachers, of their behaviours. Adults must then come together and question everything the kid tells you about how people view them. For this to work efficiently, both parties need to speak to each other directly without the child being present.

- Address the school actions of the child on a daily basis with teachers and principals.

- Establish a policy at home and at school not to rely exclusively on knowledge that your child is providing you on what others have done.

- Sit down with all caregivers (including baby sitters, grandparents, aunt, uncles) to ensure they understand Unusual and obey the policy outlined above.

- Do not involve the child with other parents in these discussions.

- Have a strategy and try not to be emotional when you respond to the actions of the kid.

- If you respond emotionally too much, you can be making major mistakes in dealing with the boy. Everyone needs to decide on what to do in advance when the child is engaging in thosebehaviours–and then be prepared to follow through calmly.

- Behavioural adjustment techniques have been widely used in ODD therapy settings, and can also be used effectively at home. The basic principle of behavioural intervention (or behavioural therapy) is that the effects will sustain actions. It indicates that old habits are resisting change because more positive effects accompany new behaviours. Many therapists agree that the trick to improving habits is to concentrate on the positive behaviours and not respond emotionally to the negative behaviours.

For behaviour change to function, certain elements must be included in the program:

- Address just a few critical habits, instead of attempting to change them all. You may want to concentrate, for example, on removing particularly offensive actions such as hitting people, cheating or swearing.

- Be very specific about the actions you'd expect. Instead of saying, "listen while I'm talking," say, "Sit down and make eye contact with me while we're talking." Be consistent—no breaking the rules in any circumstances!

- Rewards should not be money or items that are purchased for good behaviour. Instead, grant rewards which include activities the child enjoys.

- Rules should be clear and easy so that they can be easily understood. When your child is able to read, write the rules and consequences (negative as well as positive) into a contract and get it signed.

- Decide what habits to ignore.

- Many Weird kids and teenagers do so many things that you hate to include any of them in a behaviour management program. The main caregivers must determine in advance which habits are targeted for improvement, and which are simply to be ignored.

Understanding Challenging School Behaviour.

The issue of challenging behaviour is about growing concern for educators at any schooling level. Kids in today's world are going to school with elevated levels of tension and confusion in their lives. Going to school with anxieties, a history of bad early years interactions, and family challenges they carry with them a range of activities that can interfere with the learning process for themselves and others. To order to reduce the incidence and extent of behavioural disruptions to classrooms, efforts are under way to develop and maintain programs at the classroom, school and program level. Understanding the psychological, social, family, and brain-based factors that lead to disruptive behaviour is the first step towards developing successful school-wide policies and relevant instructional interventions that minimize school behavioural disruptions.

What's Challenging Behaviour?

Hard to describe difficult behaviour. It is not a disorder, and not a condition of special education (although it may accompany other conditions of special education). The educational literature does not provide a single and agreed definition, but the one in the INTO handbook is a reasonable reference point "Behaviour of such severity, frequency and length that the physical health of the individual or others is likely to be put in serious danger or behaviour that is can/likely to seriously limit or delay access to and use of ordinary facilities" The INTO paper once again offers a clear overview of the array of difficult activities experienced in schools that interfere with the learning of the pupil and/or other pupils.

Challenges the school's day to day functioning.

Challenges the right to a safe and secure atmosphere for staff and pupils.

Has a period, frequency, severity or consistency that is outside the normal range of what schools accept is less likely to respond to the regular range of measures used by the school for misconduct (INTO, Handling Challenging Behaviour) From an educational point of view, the most important point to remember is that whatever activity is classified as "challenging" is a typeo Behaviour is difficult when our actions as educators fail to will either its frequency or severity, assuming they are sufficient in the first place.

What Causes Challenging Behaviour?

Challenging behaviours, whether they occur in children, teenagers or adults, may emerge from a number of causal factors, including but not limited to o Senile Dementia, o Alzheimer's Disease, Huntington's Disease, Severe Autism, Moderate / Profound General Learning Impairment, Communication difficulties, Special education conditions, Dysfunctional family systems, Dysfunctional schools, ADHD, Traumatic Brain Injury, Schizophrenia, Bi-Polar Disorder, o Socio-economic Disadvantage, Opposition Defiant Disorder, Child temperament, Conduct Disorder, Educational neglect, Abuse, trauma, chaos, Attention-seeking, Dysfunctional teachers, Developmentally inappropriate methodology.

Considering that the cause of challenging behaviour can be varied, it is important for educators to be mindful that any approaches need to be adapted to the cause, be they at the level of classroom or school policy. Interventions for problematic behaviours that result from ADHD would likely be detrimental to the kid if administered to children with autism and lead to increased difficulties. It is not possible for this purpose to produce one-size-fits-all solutions or to provide a manual for fast fixes. It is important to examine the causal factors, analyze the causal situation, take a close look at the classroom and school setting and ensure that there is a good "match" between cause and effect before something is done to establish interventions.

Issues in Identifying Challenging Behaviour.

Because there is no commonly accepted description of what constitutes challenging behaviour, it follows that what is identified as challenging, by whom it is defined and by whom it is represented can differ greatly. All behaviour, whether environmental, social, cultural or historical, is linked to a context. In another sense, what is daunting can be viewed as very natural. The subjective complexity of human conduct makes it hard to be certain of what is acceptable or unacceptable.

Another challenge in deciding whether behaviour is challenging or not is the fact that we can not be sure on what

what we find challenging is a continuum of behaviour or a separate category of behaviour. At what exact point is a action ceasing to irritate and being challenging? Who is making the decision and how? Which are the parameters used to make the judgment? It is well known in schools that a child identified by one teacher as challenging is viewed by another as a typical youth. Like with all parents and all adults, all teachers have varying tolerance levels for behavioural variations. Until we assume that a child demonstrates troubling behaviour, we must take caution. There are times when the issue lies inside us as hard as it may be to accept, not the kid.

As causative agents in challenging behaviour, researchers try to figure out biological and environmental influences. The old nature or nurture question has now been resolved definitively. It is not the one or the other but both; it is the way our personality is nurtured that defines our behavioural repertoire to a large degree. However, there are biological factors that place an person at greater risk for behaviour that threatens growth. Those have a long family history of mental health problems, including delinquency and personality. Further of this will be said later.

Sex based problems are also involved in challenging behaviour. In the West, girls are socialized differently from boys, as in other countries. Males are played more aggressively than girls right from childhood, are encouraged to participate in more aggressive play, and have behavioural behaviours accepted differently when they occur than when they occur in females. Research seems to suggest that only one factor accounts for the difference in how father parent children then participate in their education, as opposed to mothers-the amount of physical play. Fathers prefer to play with children more vigorously than mothers, and play more vigorously with their male children than with their female children. Evidence appears to suggest that the male sex hormone plays an significant role in boys ' violent behaviour. There is yet to be a clear solution to any of those gender problems.

When trying to develop strategies, services and initiatives for children with difficult behaviours, ethical problems will often rear their heads. Which kinds of steps are necessary? Which is the Punishment Role? Are the sanctions reasonable? What habits are we going to try to change and what the child will pay if we change them successfully. Children living in their neighborhood in a violent and hostile atmosphere will pay a price if their own hostile reactions are avoided in school altogether. There are some survival factors that need to be taken into account before we try to dramatically alter children's behaviour. I'm not calling for conflict tolerance in school but attempting to raise the ethical concerns involved in having an obsessive emphasis on individual actions rather than on conduct and school systems.

Perspectives on Difficult Behaviour.

The response to challenging behaviour is affected by the behavioural perspective one takes. The behavioural viewpoint suggests that reinforcement can learn and form all behaviours. Positive enhancement increases behaviour, punishment or negative reinforcement reduces behavioural frequency. A human being is a collection of responses influenced by the external world, from the behaviourist perspective. A viewpoint on cognitive behaviour puts cognition at the root of behaviour. We behave according to our way of thought, visualizing, or imagining. Through the viewpoint, the human being is more than just a series of sensory responses, but is a conscious being, making decisions, perceiving the world in certain ways, and behaving according to the reasoning rules laid down in the brain of thought. The psychodynamic perspective conceives actions as a product of unconscious conflicts, primal forces the individual is consciously unaware of, and deep-seated fears or anxieties. Through this viewpoint we are pawns of our unconscious minds, driven and pulled beyond our consciousness by powerful powers.

From those mentioned above there's a new paradigm emerging from an alternate viewpoint. It can be referred to under a number of names but is better described as a viewpoint of a biopsychosocial type. This paradigm is holistic in that it conceives the human being as a continuum of biological, psychological, and social influences all with equal behavioural effect. Genetic and environmental events and conditions have affected the human brain in its perception of behaviour, and the resulting brain structure is what triggers any specific behaviour to arise.

If we know it or not every educator has one of those viewpoints on the actions of children. The interpretation is the experiences and our interpretation forms our responses. The more we are aware of our experience, the more we are able to change it; the more we are able to change it, the greater the potential to come to a better understanding and develop new solutions.

The Biopsychosocial View.

All behaviours are the product of brain development and genetic, economic, social, family, fitness, parenting, and hundreds, if not thousands, of miscellaneous factors in the biopsychosocial context. The human brain lies at the heart of that viewpoint. In the past 10 years alone, much has been discovered about brain development, but it is too early to generalize this knowledge and establish approaches in educational settings. A look at some of the basics may also help us understand what is happening "under the bonnet."

All the children are born with a specific constitution of disposition. This is the fundamental foundation of personality, mainly inherited. Temperament is a given and lifetime stays fairly constant. Through the course of time the habits we exhibit change, some may be hidden to lead a more stable life, but a person's particular personality does not change much. Psychologists identified several temperamental factors:

- Activity Level-how the child is usually involved.
- When not involved, distractability-degree of attention / concentration.
- Intensity-how loud that is the boy.
- Regularity-predictability of both appetite and sleep functions.

- Sensory Response to physical stimuli.

- Approach / Characteristic reaction to new situation / person.

- Adaptability-how the child adapts to transitions / new experiences with ease.

- Stubborn determination, refusal to give up.

- Mood-tendency to respond positively / negatively to work.

There is a continuum of each of these temperamental characteristics. A child may be born within the middle range of one of these or both, or may be born at the extreme end of the spectrum. All of these temperamental traits have meaning and they can all be neutral, positive or negative. Every parent with more than one child immediately identifies their children's various temperaments and slowly becomes aware of how various temperaments turn into different parenting styles. Simply put, some kids are easier to rear than others and it's the attitude that's responsible for that. Even as they can be either quick or hard to raise, children's contrasting temperamental characteristics make them harder to teach. This is nature and it is this inherent inclination of children that allows one to build environments closely matching personality at home and at school.

Why ODD Treatment Is Necessary.

Improving the connection between parent and child, which is crucial to the health and happiness of the entire family, it is important to get care. It's also important for the future of your kids. Some children will develop out of oppositional defiant disorder, while some will tend to have behavioural issues that may lead to peer alienation and difficulties in developing stable relationships, not to mention continuing family discord.

They'll also have less chance of reaching their potential. When something is not going their way, they may assume that it is the fault of someone but theirs. Dr. Anderson also says they could "retreat to the places they think they can get what they want. That may mean that they are doing even less, focusing even harder on those people who are closest to them, who they really care for most, creating even more frayed relationships.

A small number of children with Unusual tend to experience something called behavioural disorder, which is a more serious behavioural condition involving violent actions such as cheating, setting fires, and injuring people. Having diagnosed earlier rather than later increases the development of an baby.

Oppositional defiant disorder, parents play a crucial role in the treatment. It may be shocking because children are the ones with the diagnosis, but in ODD the bond between parent and child needs to be fixed, which means that both parties need to make adjustments to get back on track.

All initiatives have certain common objectives, such as helping parents find the middle ground between being too strict and too permissive. A behavioural consultant helps parents learn how to change their child's behaviour by setting realistic goals, by rewarding children when they follow through, and through using constructive punishments when they fail. Families should have to regularly follow such methods— one explanation that often behaviour modification approaches don't succeed is because families pursue new, inconsistent techniques or don't adhere to one plan long enough to make progress. Parents and children should also learn to rely on problem-solving skills when they run into problems.

Clinicians can also prescribe training in social skills to help strengthen peer interactions or cognitive behavioural therapy in your child whether it is dealing with anxiety or depression.

ODD medication is not licensed by FDA, but medicine is often used as an alternative for behavioural therapy. Anti-psychotic drugs such as Abilify (aripiprazole) and Risperdal (risperidone), which have been shown to minimize violence and irritability, are also used in situations where a child is at risk of being pulled out of school or home. Stimulant medicine can be used if an child has extreme impulsiveness like those diagnosed with ADHD. Antidepressants (SSRIs) can be effective when a child has a depression or anxiety that underlies it.

Regardless of the treatment program prescribed by your doctor, parents will have to offer a lot of support. "No mistake, children don't always just wake up unexpectedly with the realization they want their actions to be different and then ask all the adults in their lives if they can improve," warns Dr. Anderson. "We should stick to any behaviour, even though it doesn't work that well."

But once the family dynamic begins to improve, and kids (and parents) begin to feel more comfortable in their ability to get along, they will all be much happier.

Children's Bipolar Disorder-A Call for Caution.

Most health practitioners working with children and adolescents are well aware of the increase in the rate at which children and adolescents are diagnosed with Bipolar Disorder, perhaps most especially prepubescent children. Whilst figures vary from article to article, it is important to notice several statistics recently published. The New York Times, in an article/study published in September 2007, reported that there was a forty-fold rise in the rate at which this demographic was diagnosed with Bipolar Disorder in the 10-year period from 1993 to 2003, while a more scholarly study (Youngstrom, 2005) reported that there had been marked rises in the rate of diagnosis among children with Child Protective Se involvement Other scholars have pointed to this rapid rise in the pace, some favorably (NYT, 2007, Papalos and Papalos, 2006), also suggesting there needs to be an increase even further. Others, however, expressed concern at this drastic rise, and pleaded with clinicians to take a more conservative approach to pre-adult diagnosis of this. In spite of this classification, there is a lot of controversy in the field, fiercely opined views and disagreement in the field brought on by the vast difference between the most liberal, and the most conservative. This division is apparent to some degree between psychiatrists and psychologists, and indeed, the previously mentioned NY Times article pointed out that psychiatrists made 90 percent of children's diagnosis of Bipolar Disorder. Nevertheless, there are also other mental health practitioners in the area, including psychologists and other non-psychiatric folk, who follow the egalitarian approach that other psychiatrists share.

What inspires us to treat Children and Teenagers with Bipolar Disorder?

One of the most frequently cited reasons for those who support early detection is prevention: prevention of disadvantaged childhood, prevention of academic challenges, prevention of social failure, prevention of birth defects, etc. The danger, advocates of opine earlier diagnosis, is that failure to act is a disservice for the child and those interested in the life of the child. It has been the reported reason driving clinicians such as Dr. Dimitri Papalos and his wife, Janice Papalos, among others, and indeed, any specialist with some modicum of empathy has most likely acknowledged this when focusing on a potential case of Bipolar Disorder in a child or adolescent. For, if indeed allowing a child to move through their childhood without appropriate care sentences them to an understandard future, who would hesitate to act amongst us? The concern is that it's not completely clear whether we got this right, and it's most definitely not clear whether what seems to be children's Bipolar Disorder will accompany the child into adult life.

What Is This Animal We Call Childhood Bipolar Disorder?

It is widely known in adulthood that Bipolar Disorder includes discrete Panic cycles, and discrete Depression cycles. There are, of course, the murkier cases involving mixed events, but it is well-accepted that in adulthood these cases often occur. Nevertheless, as we descend into adolescence retrospectively, the waters get more muddy and more turbid. What does Early Puberty feel like Bipolar Disorder? Who happens to late prepubescence? And what about that very young guy? A analysis of the literature (Papalos and Papalos, 2006, Youngstrom, 2005, Danner-Ogston, et al, in press, Geller, 1997, etc.) shows views ranging from very conservative (let's keep things as they were) to very radical (let's diagnosis in infancy). Opinion is based in some kind of rational argument or other, but most importantly there is no consensus, and there is clear evidence to support a cautionary call.

Conservative Approach.

The cautious approach to diagnosing children with Bipolar Disorder is to keep things the way they are. In other words, in terms of frequency of symptoms and duration of moods, the child / adolescent must follow the Major Depression criterion, and for Mania. Under this strategy, the child would need to show extreme depression for one week, in most cases, and would need to disclose chronic mania for the better part of a week before being considered for treatment. Such length requirements could be waived in cases where there was considered to be a mixed episode but the severity requirements could not.

Liberal Approach.

Opinions differ in the more liberal approach, but there is a general relaxation of the standards of duration and frequency, so much so that children will move from minute to minute in the most liberal approach! In the more liberal approach, the propensity to redefine what constitutes depression or mania in children is often noted, with the most liberal approach describing mania as consisting mainly of persistent and extreme agitation, or general rage issues. Through this approach, depression can primarily manifest as frustration, or detachment from society.

Interim Conclusion.

In the opinion of some experts, the problem with the traditional approach is that we are actually missing children who deserve to have the diagnosis and care. And yes, when a kid or adolescent has serious emotional or behavioural issues and is not treated, they frequently go from bad to worse in their lives. The problem with the liberal approach is that therapy, which is driven by the medical system, requires the introduction into the child's body of potentially dangerous psychotropes. Some of the psychotropics used to treat Bipolar Disorder in children and adolescents are given' off label,' without FDA approval, and without knowledge of the possible long-term adverse effects of this medication on the developing body and brain.

Current Research.

Because of the saliency of this particular field of mental health, much or more work has been done over the last decade. NIMH, NAMI, and others have supported many studies to address questions relevant to this debate. These included the popular The Bipolar Child (Papalos and Papalos, 2006, and earlier editions), The All Parents Guide to Children With Bipolar Disorder, among others. What, instead, is the science state? How is it that we know?

According to Papalos and Papalos, there was a great deal of variation about what could be found in a child or adolescent with Bipolar Disorder in an informal research study involving interviewing parents who had classified their child as Bipolar. Papalos reported moodiness symptoms, insomnia, difficulties with sensory integration, sleep disorders, intense temperature tantrums, depression, food sensitivities, impulsivity, distractibility, anxiety, hyperactivity, oppositional characteristics, and other symptoms. Indeed, they were of the opinion that since Bipolar Disorder spanned such a spectrum of symptoms (many of which were present in other psychiatric illnesses of the youth, such as Autism, Asperger's, Oppositional Defiant Disorder, Attention-Deficit / Hyperactivity Disorder,

Posttraumatic Stress Disorder or PTSD, etc.), this condition would first be treated and additional diagnoses considered if the symptoms went While the findings of Papalos and Papalos is by far the most severe, other researchers feel that there is a need for a far more moderate understanding of what Bipolar Disorder is in adolescents, although they do not go to the lengths that Papalos and Papalos do. The assumption appears to be that children with Bipolar Disorder do not have the same frequency and length measures observed at adulthood. Some radical diagnostics suggest that children and young adults may be able to function on a regular basis and may not exhibit typical mania and may not automatically worsen their depression. Many liberal diagnostics still believe that irritability is part of what may be mania, and that Psychotic Children tend to have significant rage issues. Questions that have not been resolved unequivocally based around differential diagnosis (is it Bipolar Disorder or PTSD, or both? etc).

What if the' liberals' were correct?

When the liberal solution is up to time and study testing, then there are many kids who have been given care and treatment, understandably so, which will eliminate potential issues. Such a positive approach may also boost public awareness in the area of mental health and can improve support for mental health issues or mental health concerns identification policies.

What if the "Conservatives" are correct?

If the conservatives are right, we could have a public tragedy on our hands. Treatment with Bipolar drugs for children and young adults is unproven, often unsuccessful, and marred by the many side effects and possible long-term damage that may occur. Bipolar medications can cause anxiety, increased behavioural difficulty, moodiness, weight gain, sweating, exhaustion, and even more severe complications, such as polycystic ovarian syndrome, often fatal skin disorder, tremors, seizures, and death. It may also be that telling a child that they have less control over their emotions and actions than a normal child, or that they have no control, may cause them to give up and eventually deteriorate in their behaviours. There are also those who believe that pushing drugs on young children is a deep belief in them that medications are the solution to their ills... And how far from that is the assumption that the solution could be illegal substances?

How Are We Doing Well?

What do we do in the light of all the concerns? What do we know about the more traditional approach to diagnosis and treatment? The findings are not promising when revising the literature. Dr. March of Duke University, for example, points out that we have no idea whether children diagnosed at the age of 5 to 7 are really going to be bipolar when they are older. It is noted in the NYT article that most evidence shows that these children are more likely to have depression when they get older, rather than Bipolar Disorder. Typically speaking, it seems that drugs sometimes do not resolve the majority of the symptoms and it seems like their greatest effect is in the area of sedation, which is a double-edged sword. The kid or young adolescent in particular is more stable and less unpredictable, but they are often also less able to concentrate on learning, and can undergo significant personality changes with unintended effects on their social performance. Mood stabilisation is always an elusive target, even with strong psychopharmacological therapy, and in certain cases during pharmacological treatment the mood becomes more erratic. Additionally, side effects often become a issue in and of themselves, requiring additional medications, changes in diet, changes in learning strategies, and even improvements in the general standards of the ability of the child to work in their environment. In certain cases, the drugs make the child theoretically liable for disability insurance due to their deteriorating effects on their functioning. In certain cases, pharmacological treatments are often directed by overworked and exhausted psychiatrists of children and adolescents who can not invest the time required to thoroughly evaluate the child and his or her needs and who are also forced by pharmacological firms, explicitly and indirectly, to prescribe a specific drug or to classify a certain portion of their caseload as Bip Overall, even though one supports the idea that children and adolescents are under-diagnosed with Bipolar Disorder and that they should be treated with drugs, the end result is always partial to a complete inability to resolve the problem.

Are we missing something?

Researcher by Martin Teicher, M.D., Ph.D., (2000) indicates that early trauma, whether psychological, physical, or verbal, may have a potentially long-term impact on the developing brain. Indeed, his work indicates that such trauma, and especially (interestingly) verbal violence, has long-term effects on the corpus callosum and on the precuses, as well as on the hypothalamus, as well as on other areas. The corpus callosum is important in balancing the right and left brains, and those with underdeveloped corpus collosis appear to be highly reactive or unbalanced in their approach to problem solving (interpret: overly emotional and emotionally reactive... in other words, more likely to be angry, aggressive or irrational). People with underdeveloped precueses appear to be less rational, less cohesive in their personality and in their reactions generally inappropriate. Thus, many of the behavioural and mood problems we see in the prepubescent or post-pubescent child that arise from certain early childhood experiences, in his opinion. In other words, he's proving what doctors at the front line have been saying all along: subjecting a child to violence appears to cause them to undergo big changes in temperament, and they are frequently aggressive and emotional. When Dr. Teicher ultimately prevails, it may well be that what we thought was Childhood Bipolar Disorder was in fact a trauma condition. And the ramifications of that: the difference between potentially temporarily disabled or permanently disabled labeling of the kid.

The extent at which Childhood Bipolar Disorder develops in children and adolescents is much debated. The assumption that this is an important area to investigate, as the consequences for this condition over a person's lifetime are significant, is not controversial. Yet we need to get it right, because otherwise, then we will have undiagnosed cases that significantly alter the chances of success of the child / adolescent, or we will have medicated children unable to thrive under the weight of the side effects of excessive medicine. At the end, it's research that can clear the air... Nice, rational, replicable science that can show us what Bipolar Disorder looks like in Children, if indeed it does exist. Nonetheless, caution seems appropriate before we have a medical consensus, and the more cautious solution would be to accept other, less long-term conceptualizations of the collection of symptoms for the child.

ODD Children And Behaviour: What You Ought To Learn As A Parent.

As a parent of an ODD child, do you ever feel overwhelmed? Kimberly Abraham and Marney Studaker-Cordner have collaborated for 20 years with parents of children with Oppositional Defiant Disorder — and Kim is the parent of an adult ODD child. Read on to find out what 5 things you need to learn in order to become a more successful parent.

To raise an unusual child is like belonging to a different kind of club: it is parenting's "Special Forces Unit." If you have an ODD child, parents with "typical people" will never dream with experiencing circumstances. What is worse, for this task you have not volunteered — it's even more like being drafted. And while you do your best to parent a very hard child, you are often misunderstood by experts and other parents who raise the typical children.

It helps us remember what drives the actions of your child: the need to be in control.

In the end it's not your average kid with ODD. The Big Difference? Typical children would let others exert some degree of power over them. They can argue but ultimately they will give in. They the violate rules, but they allow for grounding themselves. They must eventually give the parental (or adult) authority over. What is the biggest fear that an Unusual kid has? Loss of influence on a parent, or any person of adult authority. Your Peculiar child will dig its heels in instead of yielding in an argument. It is on when he feels threatened! Earthed? Oh, oh! During grounding parents sometimes feel more unhappy than their child in the ODD. In the 15-year-old Jack's words, "I know how to get underground. I'm just going to turn my stereo up so loud all my mother's knick knacks are falling off the shelves. She would beg me to come out of the house!"If you're living in your home with a" Jack, "here are some tips:.

Nobody Wins the Blame Game.

It can/may be easy to fall into the pit of guilt when your home is in chaos because of endless fights with your kids. Kim is an ODD child's parent and when she raised him she sometimes found herself thinking things like, "My son is destroying my life. I have spent my whole time interacting with him. I do not even have time for myself anymore. "And she didn't blame him for how she felt and the endless turmoil in her life, she blamed herself several times. "I would torment myself by thinking,' If I were a better mom, he wouldn't be like this,'" she says. "Whenever I found myself caught up in that Blame Game, after realizing what I was doing, I was trying to take a step back and remember what I was thought. In my son or myself it was typically hurt or disappointment: I was personally taking the action or choices of my boy. I needed to understand that my son was not responsible for my emotional well-being — I was. "Blaming yourself or your child does not change the situation, and could leave you feeling frustrated and resentful towards him. To make it worse, on top of that you'll come out feeling guilty. It is good to hold your child accountable for his actions, but when it turns to blame, the feelings of resentment will only get worse. In addition, the children are eager to blame others for their own behaviour.

Instead, you want them to be a role model by taking responsibility for their own thoughts and actions.

Tug of War Gives Rope Burn to You.

It helps us remember what drives the actions of your child: the need to be in control. Faced with lack of power, ODD children often go to lengths to defend against authority. Suddenly, you no longer concentrate on the action or problem at hand; you're in a fight for power. Because of your child learning from the consequences, things get off the subject easily. You could start trying to discuss the grades of your son in kindergarten, and end up arguing over whether or not you were throwing away his Matchbox cars when he was four. Yet being involved in power struggles will leave you tired, angry and sometimes confused about what the heck has just happened! Our advice is this: Try letting go of the rope when you are in a tug-of-war over control. And ask yourself, in this debate, "What is my intention?"When you're arguing literally with no specific path or intent, it's probably not a debate that needs to take place. Only walk away is the right thing to do. Also, tugging on the string takes 2. If you keep pulling on your hand, you'll probably end up in the mud.

A reply is not needed at times. Children sometimes just need to wind down. Always need to get something out of your mind, but are you not really looking for a response? As parents, we want to step in to seek and fix what we view as problems for our children. Often when they complain or get angry, it doesn't really involve a answer from us beyond, "I hear what you're saying." Kim used to go into "fix-it" mode with her friend, offering troubleshooting solutions even if he didn't ask for guidance. Not unexpectedly, he would shoot down any suggestion of her, and then get upset with her. Why? For what? Since he just didn't want to fix anything for her.

If your child is looking for a reaction or an response, they will ask you. Otherwise, just try to listen, without jumping in to help. Let your child feel his or her emotions, and know that he has been noticed.

Keeping a tab just leaves you with an enormous Bill. With Kim's son, she says it was never that he had done "just one thing — it was that he had done twenty things over the course of a day (or sometimes an hour)." So it wasn't just that he had refused to take care of his dishes, it was that an hour before he kicked a hole in the wall, and an hour before that, he had clashed with his brother. She kept in her head a running list of everything that he had done wrong. This left her feeling lost and exhausted. She would've had enough by the time he declined to take care of the dishes. She might give you a list of offences he had committed back to the time he was six and hurled mashed potatoes against the wall only because he was bored! Yet there is another side of that coin: her son would also give her a running tab of the mistakes she would made as a mum, back to the time he thought she was selling his toys at a garage sale. It was a formula for claims, and battling for strength.

Just like parents want an opportunity to learn from our mistakes and start fresh every day, so our kids deserve the same. Although these acts are often difficult to distinguish, try to make your answers match the actual behaviour, instead of the running list you've been going through your head. In other words, do not encourage the compounding of your child's poor actions until there is no penalty or consequence that is significant enough for them.

Set a few house rules which are non-negotiable and execute with consequences. Kids with ODD also have anxiety and an intense desire to monitor their environments and others. Keep simple and restricted house rules so children don't feel stifled or frustrated. For example, rules can include, "We don't harm ourselves, others, or properties. We're using kind words and don't raise our voices." Show house rules and agree on the implications of violating a rule in advance so children know what to expect if they do. If the outcome is full for your kid, proceed from the accident. Show your kid that every new day is an opportunity to make better choices.

When coping with the actions of your kid, use a calm voice. A child with an Oppositional Defiant Disorder also wants to engage his / her parents in a will war. Explain your stance or parental obligation in as few words as possible and do not continue to address the matter. Children have trouble reasoning because they don't have anybody to disagree with them! If you engage with a stubborn child in a back-and-forth debate, you have given the child the power to handle the conversation. Know, the rules of the house apply to everyone in your household. If you break one of the rules of the house, give yourself a consequence such as apologizing or taking a brief time-out to gather your thoughts. Since children with ODD often see themselves as victims, lead by example to illustrate to your child that you are not too proud to apologize and that the rules of the house apply to all within the family.

Celebrate the successes your child has accomplished. Children with ODD have difficulty controlling their feelings, which may contribute to the disorder's extreme outbursts and tantrums. If your kid handles his or her actions effectively for a longer than usual period of time, celebrate those accomplishments with a family dinner at a favorite restaurant or some other fun family activity. Let your child know you note the extra effort, and appreciate it. Give your child time to have fun and interact when he or she is happy and working well.

Build an organized environment. It's no secret that children are better able to regulate their emotions when they're well-rested, physically fit and get enough nutrients. Give priority to exercise, balanced meals and sufficient sleep. A disciplined, healthy lifestyle will help a child with an Oppositional Defiant Disorder, as well as your entire family!

Change your Thoughts.

How you think about things defines how you feel towards your child and how you behave towards him. If your thoughts are negative, the way you communicate and react to his behaviour— and to him as a person — shall affect. See if you can grab stuff that pops into your mind, and replace it with more optimistic thinking. For instance, when "Jack" digs his heels in on something, instead of thinking, "He's so stubborn; it's just an argument," try to turn that thought into, "He's certainly determined." Changing your thoughts will help you shift how you feel about your kid.

The normal reaction when someone pushes you against is to fight back. As Kim's son pushed her in defiance she said she "always found herself pushing back in response, without even thinking about it." Your child may have the kind of personality that will continue to push against others and fight against being dominated in any way. Make no mistake, parenting an ODD child is an emotional undertaking and a challenge. It's a cycle of trying to be innovative, as you will continually search for "things that work" for a child whose very nature is struggling against power.

The fact is, the temperament of your child is unlikely to change, but if you follow these suggestions we give you can find yourself less often and less deeply involved in the conflict. As Kim says, "I had found it difficult for my child to fight in the process without a parent. Through improving the way I reacted to him, our relationship has improved over time. "If you can change the way you react to your boy, the outcome will be less tension and more harmony in your household. And you'll be teaching your child conflict management skills by modeling the strategies we've given you, de-escalating methods, positive communication skills and coping skills. Better part? You will finish the day feeling good about yourself and realizing you gave it your all.

How Brain Control Can Assist Children with ODD.

If your child displays actions linked to Oppositional Defiant Disorder or is unable to control his or her feelings in an acceptable age manner, we encourage you to try The Brain Function Programme.

Is your child destructive or does it have behavioural problems that hinder its everyday functioning? Start with our Online Preliminary Assessment Quiz!

We believe that at Brain Balance every child can be linked to success. Our Achievement Centers deliver the Brain Balance Program at more than 100 (and growing) locations nationwide.

We work with children who have SPD, ADHD, learning disabilities, OCD, Tourette syndrome and Asperger syndrome symptoms. The curriculum for every child is special to its own challenges.

Defiant Child Parenting.

Children born with a difficult temperament or other form of biological predisposition tend to be at high risk for violent and oppositional actions by parents (Frick & Morris, 2004). According to the Hawkins et al. (2000), children who exhibit early-age stubbornness, frustration, poor attitudes and issues are at an elevated risk of future psychiatric diagnosis and becoming offending adults.

As a social issue, as a childhood epidemic, the disorder of resistance, opposition and behaviour has not been centered. The emphasis was on dilemmas surrounding foster care, special education, teen pregnancy, sexually transmitted infections, drop-out rates in high school and adolescent suicides. There is witness to the lack of emphasis on resistance and oppositionalism in the gap of funding rates. The estimated cost of handling defiance in 1990 was just $15,000 per young person (Foster and Jones, 2006). This is less than the $25,000-

$40,000 spent every year on supporting a single child in foster care or residential programs.

When school-age children frequently exhibit counter-productive activities, it may disturb the entire family and school environment. An excessive desire for dominance, unreasonable levels of frustration and a general disregard for others are at the root of most destructive behaviours exhibited by children. Such and other destructive actions contribute to the child being branded as defiant. Defiant attitudes are also the by-product of certain issues occurring in a child's life. The defiance is an response or an effort to settle internal disputes.

The persistent pattern of cynicism, denial and putting blame in the therapy area is referred to as oppositional defiant disorder. The condition often includes a child's willingness to challenge limits, disregard social / family norms, disrupt other people's personal space / basic rights, defy laws, complain, harass, and turn to aggression and coercion as a means of functioning. The stubborn child is by far one of the toughest kids to parent.

Parenting Perspective:

To avoid undue degrees of anger and anxiety, parents must recognize that a child's defiance is a decision. The expectation for a parent to perform or fix the child's issues is resolved by first recognizing that the stubborn child can always prefer to be a thorn in the flesh in a "perfect world or when offered whatever it desires." The goal of parenting is not to give in or become frustrated; rather, the goal is to resolve the anger, indignation and wrath of the child.

Stages of Parenting:

Parents should take many "consistent" steps to resolve a child's defiance.

You're not alone to know.

The first or number one step parents need to take is knowing they're not alone. I find that as parents understand that they are not alone, their level of anger decreases well before better habits in the childhood are seen. I find myself reminding parents on a daily basis that "You're not alone. There are millions of good parents all over the world experiencing the same degree of child defiance." Childhood defiance is a global epidemic. In a recent survey, Rescola et al (2007) published on teacher records of 30,000 students from 21 countries having behavioural and emotional problems. The research countries included Thailand, Italy, China, Portugal, Denmark, the United States and Greece. The teachers commented on resistance, problems of thinking, social issues, perfectionism, impulsiveness, non-compliance, completion of assignments, anxiety, depression, etc. They mentioned all the kids had similar problems with the home and school.

The research study that has been referred to brings home the point that as a parent you are not the only parent to have a defiant child.

Expose The Root.

The second phase is revealing the root cause of behaviours in a child. Nobody enjoys being subjected to this. It is a really uncomfortable feeling. A good quality heart-to-heart conversation with a child about the cause and nature of its rebellion sets the stage for better childhood behaviour. The revealing act lets the child know that its "issues" have been recognized and an action plan is being created. The revealing act often means that the child is supposed to "surrender" them, and to do better.

Displace The Anger.

The third or number threestep for parents to take is to assist the child with compassion and harmony in replacing their frustration, rage and dissatisfaction. This is a vital move that can take a while to develop because defiance basically behaves and operates as though the child are "poisoned" with insatiable needs. I found that this "poisoning" involves constant and deliberate conversations with the child about moving on emotionally, not grudging, acknowledging others and their shortcomings, etc.

Getting parents to take the fourth step has consequences. Consistently applied, actions have the potential to help kids change their behaviours. Not being grounded, the loss of privileges or public humiliation are the most powerful consequences for the rebellious kid. Rather, I found effects that extend the child beyond its comfort zone are successful. I have also found that results that generate the "feeling" of guilt, regret, and apathy / empathy are effective in curbing defiant behaviours.

Parent Training.

The fifth measure that parents need to take is providing more preparation. I find that parent preparation and new knowledge securing accounts for more than 30 per cent of the childhood defiance solution. An effective parent training program, according to Kazdin and Whitley (2006) and Hughes and Obeldobel (2007), provides guidance and exercises on problem-solving, parental adjustment, and marital / single-hood satisfaction.

Enrolling in programs for parental preparation is a challenging decision for parents to take. Many parents describe like an act as humiliating, needless, filled with false promises beneath them. I thought that might or may not be valid. This is only fair, however, that if driver's education courses, ministerial training, and life guard courses are a required "evil" and help to provide skills, then certainly a parenting class here and parents will benefit.

I also found myself delivering single-on - one parenting lessons for sensitive situations. Those intensive and often successful sessions tend to concentrate on the parent's own level of depression, childhood trauma, stressors, communication style, etc.

The most complicated possibly is the sixth step for parents to take. In order to effectively parent and overcome the resistance and oppositionalism of a child, parents must tackle socio-economic obstacles such as poverty and inadequate housing. The defiant child wants to see their parents making concerted efforts to break the hold and sting of income insufficiency, inadequate accommodation, constant activity, dysfunctional parental relationships, abuse and crime.

Kids with an Oppositional Defiant Disorder Discipline.

It is a major challenge to raise a child with an oppositional defiant disorder. Kids with oppositional defiant disorder complain about, fail to follow orders and take joy in deliberately offending others. Parenting these kids therefore needs a somewhat different disciplinary approach.

Kids with an oppositional defiant disorder can be smart, imaginative, and compassionate given their behavioural issues. And their actions can change over time with the aid of supportive parenting strategies.

Establish a Behaviour Plan.

Establish a behaviour plan to resolve the particular behavioural issues of your child such as violence, talking back, failure to do homework, or throwing temper tantrums.

Identify the effect your child will get when she violates the law. Explain in detail the repercussions for her.

Additionally, explore the beneficial results that she receives when he shows good behaviour. Reward systems can be very useful tools for children with oppositional defiant disorder, particularly token economy systems.

Set Simple Rules.

Children with oppositional defiant disorder enjoy fighting over laws. If things don't seem equal, they look for loopholes and show concern.

Reduce any claims by setting down simple guidelines for households. Post the refrigerator rules or other prominent position inside the building.

Then, check the list as required. When your child says, "I don't want to do my homework right now," they point out, "The rules say homework time starts at 4:00." Keep the rules clear and don't make the list too long. Include clear rules on topics like homework, chores, bedtime and respect.

Avoid Power Struggles.

Kids with oppositional defiant disorder are excellent at luring grown-ups into long debates. But taking steps to prevent power struggles is necessary, since they are not helpful or successful.

When you're asking your child to clean his room, and he's arguing with you, resist the complaint. The longer he traps you in an argument, the more he stops his room cleaning. Provide him explicit orders instead, and offer a penalty if he decides not to follow through.

Don't try to push anything on your kids. You can not keep his room tidy. You can't force him to do the homework. Arguing, nagging, and yelling doesn't work.

However, if he wants not to do as you've suggested by showing him repercussions, you will make it difficult for him. When he doesn't do what you told him, give him a message that explains precisely what will happen if he doesn't do what you're doing.

Say, "If you don't get off the device right now, you're going to lose your computing privileges for the next 24 hours." If after a few seconds he doesn't comply, follow through with the effect.

Be Consistent With The Consequences.

Kids with oppositional defiant disorder need to have clear punitive consequences for misbehaviour.2 When you occasionally let your kid get away with violating the law, he won't grow.

When he knows there's one in a hundred chance you're going to break down and give in when he argues, he's going to decide it's worth a shot. So, over time, he can become more argumentative.

Grant Positive Attention.

Kids with an oppositional defiant disorder appear to grate on the nerves of individuals. Therefore many of their adult experiences are negative. They get more orders, rebukes and consequences than other children.

Regular doses of positive reinforcement can be crucial to avoiding issues with behaviour. Play games together, ride out or do a project together. Regardless of how your child has acted on the day, give him at least 15 minutes of undivided attention.

Positive attention to your child1 will every his attempts to grab your attention by negative behaviour. So find the expenditure in quality time in rising long-term behavioural issues.

Get Help.

When your child is not consistently receiving medical support, you may want to discuss it. Parental counseling is also a significant part of treatment1 and at home, a trained psychologist will assist you with behaviour management strategies.

Community groups can be helpful too. It can be overwhelming to raise a child with an oppositional defiant disorder and it is helpful to talk with other parents who understand.

Educate yourself about oppositional defiant disorder, as soon as you can. Understanding it can be necessary to help a child develop new skills to control their behaviour.

Healing Our Families Through Attachment Parenting And Natural Education In An Industrialized Society

-Mahatma Gandhi.

Our society has shifted away from the way nature planned for us to become parents and take care of our children. Unfortunately, people have lost contact with their innate parental instincts for many years as the world has become more and more industrialised. In a way that causes anxiety, pain, depression and rage, each generation is parented. This in turn causes every new generation to transmit unhealthy ways of parenting which reflect their hurt, distress and resentment.

Alarms in nature.

Nature has designed warning signals into each animal to inform parents, partners and predators that the animal feels or detects a need, threat or risk. In nature animal parents respond instinctively to their young's alarms immediately. The warning signal of a human child is crying which is intended to alert parents to a need. When children grow older, when their needs are not met their warning signals become more complex and frequently include actions that parents find troubling.

Some of the children's alarms:

• Outbursting, • Pouting, • Tantruming, • Screaming, • Avoidance, • Clinging, • Defensiveness, • Fidgeting, • Depression, • Anxiety, • Telling us explicitly that they are in need, • Requesting us to support them fulfill their needs, • Informing them rudely, • Oppositional, • Threatening, • Disobedience, • Resisting, • Indifference, • Sarcasm, • Hyperactivity, • Scream, • Moaning, • Screaming, • Raging, • Distractibility, • Destructiveness (vandalism, breaking things, stealing, etc.), Threatening, • Aggression & violence towards people as well as animals (verbal, sexual, physical,), • Self destructiveness (self mutilation, sexual promiscuity, suicidal gestures, substance use, bad relationships, etc.), • Passive compliance, • Challenging.

The panic cries and adolescent acting-out behaviours, such as a child's screams and animal behavioural signs, are warning signals dependent on nature. Our warning signals alert us that they are physically or emotionally disturbed by something in the child's body, immediate situation, life or environment and risk our optimum growth. Our warning signals alert us that they are physically or emotionally disturbed by something in the child's body, immediate situation, life or environment and risk our optimum growth.

When we truly understand that actions are children's internal warning signs, we are less likely to threaten, medicate or manipulate children into adhering to distressing, unhealthy situations in good conscience. When we look around our culture, we will begin to understand more and more that from the hyperactive kid to the psychotic 17-year-old, discipline, coercion, incentives, intimidation and medicine don't make troubled kids happy, cooperative or compassionate; nor do those responses fill the voids and satiate the needs of kids trying to alert us with their warning signals.

—————•◆•—————

A Happy Kid Recipe: Safe parent-child relationship by meeting the needs of our children.

Kids of all ages ought to have a stable parent-child relationship to succeed. A secure-parent child relationship is essential for the optimum functioning of a child in all areas of its development. It is the blueprint and foundation for the physical, mental, financial, intellectual, cultural, spiritual and moral functioning of a child's long existence. This is the blueprint and the foundation of the future success and capacity of a child to deal with life and relationships.

A stable parent-child relationship grows from infancy to young adulthood as a result of parents fulfilling child's basic physical and emotional needs, and then the higher level needs.

That natural parenting role is part of the process of human attachment:.

- The child feels a need, whether physical or mental.
- The child communicates the need using a symbol such as to scream, demonstrate, question or say.
- As soon as possible the parent meets the need of the kid.
- The child feels relaxed, satiated, homeostasis, happiness and trust in the parent each time the child's needs are met.

Safe connection grows and evolves as a result of the unbroken cycle.

If parents typically fail to meet the needs of their child or typically postpone doing so, the parents may feel pain, anger, sadness, anxiety and mistrust in their child. That unmet need grows and strengthens and creates an unstable or disrupted connection. If a child suffers from a broken relationship, emotional and/or behavioural issues may occur immediately or begin to emerge gradually over a period of time.

Parenting and teaching nature in its intended manner.

People who live in peaceful tribal societies and non-human animals are the natural models that can show us how nature meant us to become parents. People are found to be parents in tribal societies where aggression is very small and mental disorder is generally a rarity, in line with the majority of our closest mammal relatives. Natural parenting has the most critical features:

Kid daily skin-to-skin touch and non-stop holding for the first 12 months of life.

- Breastfeeding for at least 2.5 years and optimally for up to 4 and 1/2 years.
- Kids and young children co-sleep.
- Responding to children's physical and emotional needs in infancy.
- High levels of physical intimacy, social bonding and childhood cuddling.
- Discipline and instruction which are peaceful, democratic.
- Good connections with family and friends.
- Consistent family and group modeling of action that is respectful, compassionate, interdependent (everyone does their part to support the whole).

- Natural education by play, experimentation, imitation, self-directed learning, physical activity and active community involvement; and

- Encouraging children to grow, learn and evolve at their own pace.

Some of our mammalian relatives display similar forms of parenting, especially mammals who carry their young or have regular physical contact with them, such as bonobos, gorillas, elephants and dolphins.

Child development.

As children progress through life, they face certain tasks of growth at every point of their lives. A stable parent-child relationship and natural education help them solve and complete their developmental tasks to an acceptable stage, without being hurried or coerced.

School and day care damages strong relationship between parent and child.

One of the most life-changing changes to the relationship between parent and child is when the children are put in daycare, nursery and grade school. Traditional school environments are also harmful:

Connection to parent-child involvement, Democracy, Natural growth of a kid, Intellectual growth and imagination, Body and wellbeing of the child, Social development, and Emotional and behavioural stability.

Day care and childcare divides children at age from mothers because it is vital to the growth of the brain that young children are with their families. Older adolescents are often depressed, lonely, irritated and in school emotionally drained during late adolescence. They have no time for the high-energy physical activity, creativity, inventiveness, and play they need to build their brain optimally. Furthermore, homework takes away children's attention from their own interests and from family and friends. In addition, many children are negatively influenced by their peers at the school and at younger and younger ages move away from their parents.

But school isn't good for kids?

Quick all in the "one size fits all" conventional school setting is contradictory to what nature intended for the growth of a kid. Two of the reasons the traditional school inhibits the natural growth of children are:

- Conventional schools are built to monitor large numbers of people so that they all do the same.

- The structure and curriculum of traditional schools are not in line with the developmental or learning needs of children of any generation.

- Public schools cut back on the very forms children learn and enjoy themselves: play, sports, drama, fun events, painting, music, field trips and hands-on activities.

- Conventional schools do not take into account that the main way children learn is through play and exploration. Essentially, schools depend on getting kids to sit and listen.

- Conventional school does not encourage children to direct their own learning on the basis of interests, abilities, passions and skills;

- Traditional school marks children who are unable to adapt as "ordinary learners" or "behavioural issues."

- Compulsory schooling is responsible for the exuberance, frustration or developmentally impaired learning environment of thousands of children who are prescribed medications.

- Traditional school regiments provide basic physical needs for children (food, water, nutrition, physical activity and rest) and fail to allow them to meet their own needs.

- Nearly half of the US states also allow teachers to legally attack children with paddles at public schools.

- Modern school isolates children from their families and communities;

- Children are obliged to do homework after being confined to education for six hours or more.

- Homework further isolates children from family time, time for recreation, social interaction and freedom to follow their own interests.

- Standardized examinations are structured to assess how well a child performs tasks and how well a child can recall isolated information. It does not demonstrate the intelligence, intellect, experience, imagination or moral growth of a child.

- It is believed that learning is about "finding the right answer" rather than the method of how to ask questions and where to find responses.

- Traditional school does not encourage children to have the ability to divide themselves into exclusive groups or cliques, in order to build a false sense of control.

- The control-based methods of traditional schools give no space for children's aspirations, expectations, thoughts and needs to be articulated, leading some to anger, revolt and vengeance.

- Traditional school does not work as a democracy to educate children to become active in a democratic society.

- Traditional school is an obsolete structure focused on the industrial work ethic of the late 1800's and early 1900's; and

- Traditional school has failed to adapt to meet the children's artistic and academic needs.

There are many positive alternatives to conventional school that also encourage kids to achieve learning capacity and success well beyond the range of traditionally schooled peers. Alternatives include:

• Unschooling (child-led curriculum), • Homeschooling, • Democratic schools (which are run as democracies), • Montessori schools, • Waldorf schools, • Private schools that value play, outdoor time, children's natural growth and learning pleasure, • Community charter schools (which focus on the arts and play) • Virtual (online) public or private schools, • Academic research.

Parents are continually programmed to embrace and live with too many values, patterns, behaviours, rituals and activities that seem innocuous but are actually detrimental to the normal development of children. Including:

- The manner in which our society treats children as property and as less than human compared with how adults are perceived.

- The manner in which parents and schools teach and model abuse, dominance and injustice to children by punishing them, disrespectfully speaking to them, using power techniques with them and dictating what they are going to do, where they are going to be, how they have to act and what they have to think throughout their whole childhood.

- The self-centered, materialistic, academic-obsessed, work-obsessed, sex-obsessed, money-obsessed, media-obsessed and violence-accepting ideals of parents and children's culture model of how to live; and, • The manner in which parents surround themselves with all sorts of distractions that do not meet children's needs, such as daycare, education, school sports teams, television, video games, mobile phones, etc.

Such values, patterns, and behaviours may include pressuring youth to grow up in ways that are not suitable for their growth, and refusing to naturally encourage youth to grow and develop.

Child trauma and PTSD.

Most children in our society are suffering from depression and post-traumatic stress disorder effects from distressing and frightening care such as physical discipline, and serious neglect and negligence. Trauma affects every aspects of a child's life, and ultimately rewires the brain of the infant, creating misdiagnosed emotional issues. Trauma is thought to be stored in parts of the brain which prevent it from being healed by therapy, maturity, learning and experience, causing symptoms to last for decades. A special form of therapy, called EMDR, can help to treat trauma.

Trauma Examples:

- Forcing him to go to classes.
- A lack of assistance in cases of disruption, death, sickness or other trauma.

- Placement outside the home (foster care, community home, juvenile boot camp or detention centre).

- Hard childbirth.

- Infant left in incubator to scream after conception.

- Compulsion.

- Parents who fail to respond instantly to their infant's cries.

- Crib sleeping.

- Kid left at night, alone.

- Having neglected or refused basic needs.

- Physical misconduct, including spanking, smacking, paddling, or rough child handling.

- Sexual abuse.

- Emotional abuse.

- Disregard for physical and emotional needs;

- Abandonment.

- Left to day care.

- Loss of family or loved ones.

- Death of a parent or a loved one.

- Testifying against domestic abuse.

- Witnessing abuse of some sort, or harming a human or animal.

- Harassment by colleagues.

- Victim of racial or derogatory remarks about the nationality, gender, sexual orientation or appearance of the victim.

- Aches or sickness.

- Born opioid abuser.

- Hospitalization.

- No-homes.

- Seeing TV shows, videos, games or websites that are frightening, abusive or sexualised.

Extreme Breaks In Attachment: Foster Care, Adoption and Institutional Facilities.

Children who have been adopted or who live in orphanages, foster homes, institutions and facilities often experienced severe loss of attachment, as a result of which they also often significant emotional and behavioural issues. Those are the kids who have disappointed our society, because they are among the most broken and suffering people in our communities.

Our kids have no brain defects-Our society is disordered!

Many children who act out their anger in our society are misdiagnosed with mental conditions and brain disorders such as ADHD, learning disabilities, bipolar disorder, and oppositional defiant disorder. When diagnosed, they are frequently required to take strong, mind-altering medicines. Nevertheless, most of the symptoms presented by these kids are in fact signs of a broken relationship, a developmentally dysfunctional educational environment and post-traumatic stress disorder. Though our society treats these children as "brain disordered," our society is actually disordered. Children being treated and medicated does not cure the causes of their pain. The signs displayed by children are indeed normal responses to unhealthy and intolerable circumstances in life!

Attachment repair and trauma healing.

Parents should repair the attachment and restore distress for children of all ages! Simple therapeutic values such as physical intimacy, empathizing and showing kindness to our children, plus getting support for ourselves, are vital aspects of reparing attachment and trauma. Certain provisions include:

- **Parental attachment.**

   Family values, self-discipline and accountability are instilled by positive instruction and good modeling.

- To study nonviolent ways of emotional interaction and communication with adolescents, such as the Nonviolent

Communication (NVC) model by Marshall Rosenberg or the S.A.L.V.E. method by Naomi Aldort.

- To consider alternatives to conventional education such as non-school, homeschooling, cooperative schools, Montessori schools, Waldorf schools, early schools or private schools that value play, growth of children and learning joy.
- EMDR treatment to treat trauma.
- Brain-retraining neurofeedback.
- Natural attachment therapy to help in removing dangerous attachments.
- Managing imbalances (EFT, homeopathy, etc.), therapeutic and body-centered treatments;
- To know about the risks of diagnosing and medicating actions in children.

Re-parenting children with serious damage of attachment.

Only children who have been adopted or children suffering from serious disruption of attachment or Reactive Attachment Disorder will recover and develop to firmly attach themselves to their parents! To start this very difficult process, parents have to make a lifelong commitment to their children, secure a support network for themselves and find an attachment specialist.

Parents must be able to provide re-parenting opportunities to their children that fulfill the unmet early developmental needs of their children including strong physical affection. Parents need to have a clear set of family values in place, and understand how to use consequences and redress so they don't punish their kids. To help their children develop emotional maturity each family member should learn and practice strategies for peaceful emotional communication. Adoptive parents of children with extreme disturbance of attachment should expect intense testing activities and periods of relapse as children develop to deeper and deeper attachment stages.

Healing our culture now.

The society/culture is the composite body of the values and behaviour of human generations, including ourselves, who have separated themselves from normal ways of living and parenting. Our society is very mentally ill, and disordered by "spirit!" Yet what our society wants is not a giant bottle of Adderoll, Celexa or Risperdol...

Abuse and rage saturate our culture, contributing to contempt for other human beings, disregard for all living creatures and contempt for our natural environment. Our society is obsessed with guilt over sexuality and the human body, which contributes, on the one hand, to rigid, uptight prohibitions on sexuality and, on the other hand, a persistent fascination and adolescent-like ridicule. Every generation transfers this disease of violence, guilt and anger on to the next generation, generating materialism, self-obsession, money obsession, labor obsession, academic obsession, drug obsession, media obsession and war obsession. This does not deter further services, jails, colleges, regulations, drugs, laws and punishments. We have to start by encouraging people to think differently and to feel different.

Parents, educators and lawmakers must prioritize the healing of our children and our young people, rather than labeling, punishing, medicating, confining and incarcerating them, in order for our community to heal itself. As people, we all have a duty to engage in requesting that priority be given to mental health providers, social workers, physicians, scientists, the human services departments in our state and our state legislators:

- Meeting the needs of all children right now.
- Healing the harm already done on children.
- Helping and mentoring young adults with trauma experience to prevent the next generation from suffering harm.

"You can never know what effects your action will bring, but there will be no outcome if you do nothing"

-Mahatma Gandhi.

Dyadic Developmental Psychotherapy- An Evidence Based Intervention for Attachment Problems.

Dyadic Developmental Psychotherapy is an evidentiary and effective method of care for children with trauma and attachment disorders. This is an evidential method, meaning scientific work has been conducted in peer-reviewed journals. Craven & Lee (2006) determined that DDP is a funded, appropriate treatment (in a six-level scheme, category 3). Nevertheless, their analysis only included findings from a partial preliminary presentation of a continuing follow-up study, which was later completed and published in 2006. This initial research contrasted DDP outcomes with other types of treatment,' normal care,' 1 year after completion of treatment.

It is important to remember that more than 80 percent of the study children had more than three previous episodes of therapy, but without any change in their symptoms and behaviour. Treatment episodes involve a course of treatment, consisting of at least five hours, with other mental health providers at other facilities. A second study expanded those findings to four years after the completion of the procedure. Based on the classifications of Craven & Lee (Saunders et al. 2004), the inclusion of these studies should have contributed to the classification of DDP as evidence-based category 2,' Supported and possibly successful.' There were two related longitudinal studies contrasting the results of Dyadic Developmental Psychotherapy treatment with a control group. This is the basis for the category two ranking. The parameters will be:

- In widely accepted psychological concepts the therapy has a strong theoretical basis. The Attachment Theory is based on Dyadic Developmental Psychotherapy.

- There is a significant scientific, anecdotal literature showing the effectiveness of the procedure for at-risk children and children in foster care.

- In clinical practice, the therapy is widely accepted for at-risk children and foster children. As evidenced by the vast number of Dyadic Developmental Psychotherapy professionals, and its presentation over the past ten or fifteen years as various international and national conferences.

- There is no clinical or scientific evidence or theoretical rationale to conclude-that care poses a significant risk of harm to those who seek it, compared with its possible benefits.

- The treatment has a manual which clearly defines the treatment's components and administration characteristics which require implementation. Such material is the development of attachment power, the building of attachment bonds, and attachment-focused family therapy.

- At least two studies using some type of control without randomization (e.g., waiting list, untreated community, placebo community) have calculated the efficacy of the treatment over time, the effectiveness of the treatment over placebo, or have found it to be equal to or better than a treatment already developed.

- If several treatment outcome trials were performed, the cumulative weight of evidence supported the treatment's efficacy.

Such findings support some of the assumptions and guidelines about care of O'Connor & Zeanah. They note (p. 241) that "treatments for children with attachment problems should be supported only when they are evidence-based." A qualified, well-trained, certified specialist must offer Dyadic Developmental Psychotherapy as in any other care. A family-focused diagnosis is Dyadic Developmental Psychotherapy.

Dyadic Developmental Psychotherapy is the term for an method and a set of concepts that have proven to be successful/effective in helping children with trauma and attachment problems heal; that is, maintaining safe, trusting and stable relationships with caregivers. Treatment is based on 5 fundamental concepts.

Significant and severe memories of neglect, violence, or persistent and unresolved pain in the first few years of life are at the center of Reactive Attachment Disorder. Such events disturb the usual attachment cycle to weaken or remove the child's ability to develop a safe and stable relationship with a caregiver. The child lacks a sense of confidence, health and security. The infant creates a world negatively working paradigm in which:

- Adults are found to be inconsistent or harmful.

- The planet is known as chaotic.

- The child has no powerful world impact.

- The child just wants to depend on him / her own self.

- The child feels an intense sense of guilt, the child feels damaged, negative, nasty and evil.

Reactive Attachment Disorder is a severe developmental condition triggered during the first couple of years of life by a prolonged history of maltreatment. Mental health workers who do not have the requisite qualifications and experience identifying and treating these children and adults are frequently misdiagnosed with Reactive Attachment Disorder. Children also have a number of previous problems in the child welfare system. As a consequence of disordered attachment, the habits and symptoms that are the basis for these prior conditions are best conceptualised. Oppositional actions in defiant disorder are subsumed under the Reactive Attachment Disorder. The signs of post-traumatic stress disorder are the product of a long history of violence and neglect, and are another aspect of attachment disorder. Problems of concentration and even signs of Psychotic Disorder are also seen in children with disorganized attachment.

Approximately 2 percent of the population is adopted, with signs of attachment disorder between 50 and 80 percent of these children. Some of these children become violent and disruptive and are at risk of developing a variety of psychiatric and personality disorders as adults, including antisocial personality disorder, narcissistic personality disorder, borderline personality disorder, and psychopathic personality disorder. Neglected children are at risk of social isolation, social alienation and widespread failure feelings. Children with history of violence and neglect are at high risk for adult post-traumatic stress disorder. Children that have been sexually exploited run a substantial risk of having anxiety disorders (2.0 times the average), major depressive disorders (3.4 times the average), alcohol abuse (2.5 times the average), substance abuse (3.8 times the average), and antisocial behaviour (4.3 times the average) (MacMillian, 2001). Such children are effectively regarded as a public health problem (Walker, Goodwin, & Warren, 1992).

Left untreated, abused and neglected children who have an attachment disorder become adults whose capacity to establish and sustain stable relationships is severely impaired. The disease can get worse without putting in a suitable permanent home and successful care. Most children with attachment problems develop as adults borderline personality or antisocial personality disorder.

First Principal. The treatment needs to be experiential. Because the origins of the attachment problems arise pre-verbally, counseling needs to establish therapeutic experiences. Experiences are one "active ingredient" in the healing process and not words.

Good therapy uses interactions to assist the health, protection, acceptance, empathy and emotional attunement of a child within the family. A variety of approaches and strategies are used, including psychodrama, Therapy-compatible treatments, and other activities.

Second Principal. Family emphasis will be on the counseling. Therapy helps the child resolve the underlying trauma in a "titrated" and manageable doses compassionate, healthy, stable atmosphere so that what the parents have to give will get in and heal the child. It is the ability of the parents to create a safe and nurturing home which provides a healing environment. Feeling empathy for the child, respecting the child, loving the child, being curious about the child and being playful are all part of the "attitude" that heals. The parents engage fully in the diagnosis.

Third Principal. You have to tackle the pain directly. Therapy facilitates healing by ensuring protection and safety to allow the child to re-experience the traumatic and shameful feelings surrounding the trauma of the accident. Revisiting the trauma is necessary if the child is to start revising the personal narrative and world-view of the child. The child may integrate the trauma into a coherent self by revisiting the trauma and sharing the anger and shame with an supportive, empathetic person.

Fourth Principle. There needs to be a robust safety and security climate. Traumatized children are frequently hyper-vigilant, insecure and deeply distrustful. A consistent, safe and secure environment is key to the development of the interactions the child needs to heal. This environment needs to be present at home and in therapy. One essential aspect of successful care is good communication and cooperation between the home, education, and therapy. "Compression-wraps," aggressive and intrusive stimuli designed to elicit indignation, "re-birthing," and other suggestive methods are not part of Dyadic Developmental Psychotherapy. Such intrusive and aggressive methods are not rehabilitation, are not rehabilitation, and have no place in a professional system of treatment.

Fifth Principal. Therapy is voluntary, rather than coercive. In our centre, we are very clear that physical restraint is not therapy and is not being used in any manner of care. Treatment is given in a way consisting of the Society for the Treatment and Education of Children's White Paper on Treatment Coercion.

The therapist must be well trained, qualified and have extensive expertise in treating children with disordered trauma-attachment. The Organization for the Care and Instruction of Infant Attachment, Connect, is a valuable tool for finding these therapists. You will look for the following when choosing a therapist:-

- Extensive preparation from a recognized training programme. Ask where and how long ago the therapist was trained, and for how long.
- Continuing education. Say when the therapist attended the last training session, and how long the exercise was.

- State certification within a defined specialty of mental health.

- Admission to ATTACh.

- A complete, informed consent document and related releases.

- An initial assessment to establish a strategy for differential diagnosis and treatment;

Decription Detailed For Treatment.

Daniel Hughes, Ph.D., advances Dyadic Developmental Psychotherapy (Hughes, 2008, Hughes, 2006, Hughes, 2003). Hughes explains the fundamental concepts and sums them up as follows:.

- A emphasis on own attachment techniques for both the caregivers and the therapists. Previous work (Dozier, 2001, Tyrell 1999) has shown the significance of the state of mind of caregivers and clinicians for the effectiveness of the treatments.

- The therapist and caregiver are adjusted to the individual perspective of the child and convey it back to the child. The therapist and caregiver help the child control affect and create a cohesive autobiographical narrative in the course of establishing an intersubjective attuned link with the infant.

- Sharing of interactions of subjection.

- The use of Speed and Position is important for cure.

- The unavoidable misattunions and disputes that occur in interpersonal relationships are discussed directly.

- Caregivers use interventions which promote the attachment.

- Numerous techniques, including cognitive-behavioural approaches, are used.

Interventions of Dyadic Developmental Psychotherapy emerge from many theoretical and scientific lineages. The theory of attachment (Bowlby, 1980, Bowlby, 1988), provides the theoretical basis for Dyadic Developmental Psychotherapy. Early trauma disrupts the usually evolving attachment structure by producing skewed internal selves, others and caregivers working models. It is one reason for diagnosis beyond the need for prompt care. As O'Connor & Zeanah (2003, p. 235) said, "A more puzzling case is that of an adoptive / foster caregiver who is' adequately' sensitive but the child displays an attachment disorder behaviour; enhancing parental sensitive responsiveness (in already sensitive parent) would seem unlikely to produce significant improvements in the parent-child relationship."

Current organizational behavioural theory and work on neurobiology (Siegel, 1999, Siegel, 2000, Siegel, 2002, Schore, 2001) is yet another aspect of the basis on which Dyadic Developmental Psychotherapy rests.

The primary approach is to build a stable treatment base (using strategies that align with maintaining a healing PACE (Playful, Acceptant, Curious, and Empathic) and at home using principles that provide a healthy environment and a healing PLACE (Playful, Caring, Acceptance, Curious, and Empathic). Developing and sustaining an attuned relationship where dependent mutual contact takes place helps the child recover. Coercive techniques such as rib-stimulation, holding a child in frustration or inducing an emotional reaction, shaming a child, using fear to achieve compliance, and power / control and submission-based approaches, etc., are rarely used and are incompatible with therapy grounded in attachment theory and existing understanding of interpersonal behavioural neurobiologies.

As practiced at The Center for Family Development, Dyadic Developmental Psychotherapy uses two-hour sessions involving one therapist, parent(s) and infant. There are two offices which are used. When the caregivers are in the treatment area, the caregivers have a closed circuit T.V. view of treatment from another space. Or just a one-way mirror. There are three elements to the normal layout of a session. First, once the child is sitting in the therapy area, the therapist meets the caregivers in one space. The caregiver is trained in the techniques of attachment parenting during this phase of the therapy (Becker-Weidman & Shell (2005) Hughes, 2006). It is also possible to discuss and overcome the caregiver's own issues that may cause challenges with developing affective attunement with their infant. For children with trauma-attachment disorders, successful parenting approaches include a high degree of structure and continuity, along with an affective atmosphere that reflects playfulness, curiosity, affection, acceptance, and empathy (PLACE). Caregivers provide help during this phase of the care and are provided the same degree of personalized attention we wish the child to feel. Caregivers too frequently feel accused, devalued, inept, drained and frustrated. Parent support is an essential aspect of therapy to help parents be in a stronger position to maintain an attuned relationship with their child. Third, the caregivers therapist visits the child in the therapy room. It typically takes 1 1/2 hours to complete. Third, without the infant, the therapist meets with carers. Under general terms, child care uses three types of interventions: affective attunement, cognitive rehabilitation, and psychodramatic re-enactment. Treatment with carers uses two types of interventions: firstly, to teach appropriate methods of parenting and to help caregivers prevent power struggles and, secondly, to establish a proper Position.

Child therapy has a major non-verbal aspect because a large part of the abuse happened at a pre-verbal level and is therefore dissociated from clear memory. As a consequence, childhood maltreatment and subsequent trauma build obstacles to those children's productive involvement and care. Treatment strategies are intended to build protection and affective attunement interactions such that the child is affectively involved and is able to discuss and overcome past traumas. This affective attunement is the same mechanism used during attachment promoting connections for non-verbal contact between a caregiver and child (Hughes, 2003; Siegel, 2001). The attunement of the therapist and caregivers results in the consequence of the child being co-regulated such that it is manageable. The cognitive rehabilitation approaches are intended to help the child develop secondary mental representations of stressful events that allow the child to process these events and create a cohesive autobiographical narrative. Treatment requires several repetitions of the traditional caregiver-child bonding process. The cycle starts with mutual affective interactions, followed by an violation of the relationship (a breakup or discontinuity), and concludes with an affective states reattune. Non-verbal communication, which includes eye contact, voice tone, touch and movement, are important elements for establishing affective attunement.

The treatment provided often adhered to a structure with several dimensions. First, it defines and discusses behaviours. The actions may have happened in the immediate encounter, or in the past at some point. The behaviour is examined through interest and acceptance. Second, the behaviour is investigated using curiosity and acceptance and the sense starts to emerge for the infant. Third, empathy is used to decrease the child's sense of guilt and to increase the child's sense of acceptance and understanding. Therefore, Next, behaviour of the child is standardized. In other words, if the meaning of the behaviour is known and its origin in prior trauma, the condition is understandable.

Fifth, this understanding is conveyed to the caregiver by the child.

Sixth, eventually, a new interpretation for the conduct is identified and the behaviours of the infant are transformed into a cohesive autobiographical narrative by the disclosure to the caregiver of the new experience and purpose.

Reading papers and using psychodramatic reenactments recreate past traumas. Such approaches, which take place within a secure, balanced environment, allow the child to incorporate past traumas and understand past and current interactions that generate the emotions and thoughts associated with behavioural disruptions of the child. The infant creates secondary representations of these events, emotions, and thoughts resulting in better control of the consequences and a more coherent autobiographical narrative.

The therapy, as defined by Hughes (2006, 2003), is an involved, modulated process involving acceptance, interest, empathy and playfulness. Through co-regulating the changing affective states of the infant and creating secondary representations of thoughts and emotions, the child's capacity to participate in a trustworthy relationship is strengthened. The carers follow the same values. If the caregivers find it challenging to communicate with their child in this way, therefore the caregiver's treatment is suggested.

Children with severe maltreatment and consequent complex abuse are at high risk for a number of other mental, neuropsychological, cognitive, social, interpersonal, and psychobiological conditions (Cook, A., et. al., 2005; van der Kolk, B., 2005). Children and adolescents with complex trauma need a treatment approach which focuses on multiple dimensions of disability (Cook, et al., 2005). Chronic violence and the resulting complex trauma cause disability in a number of critical areas including:-

- self-regulation.
- Interpersonal interaction like faith and comfort capability-Connection.
- Biology which results in somatization.
- Affect regulation.
- Increased use of mechanisms of defense, such as dissociation.
- Regulation of behaviours.
- Mental roles, including treatment management, motivation control and other executive functions.
- Self-belief.

Dyadic Developmental Psychotherapy addresses those disability areas. With effective, stable social casework and clinical practice, Dyadic Developmental Psychotherapy shares many essential elements. For example, caring for the client's integrity, compassion for the perspectives of the client, and beginning where the client is, are both time-honored concepts of clinical practice and they are also fundamental elements of Dyadic Developmental Psychotherapy.

ODD And ADHD.

For children with ADHD, there is a very large correlation that is often diagnosed with ODD. The range may be 30 to 50 percent of children with ADHD who have ODD, depending on the research.

Dr. Anderson describes the relation like this: "Children with ADHD are programmed biologically to be distractible, to be impulsive, to have a little trouble remaining in one position. When children with ADHD start doing things parents consider as off limits. And then when those children receive negative feedback they tend to become much more negatively focused towards adults. "These repetitive patterns of negative experiences may lead to ODD growth.

But another way to grow Unusual has more to do with the personality of a child and could be evident early on. Children who have had a lot of trouble controlling themselves as children who who have an age-appropriate ability to regulate their emotions when faced with frustration or rage may sometimes grow ODD. Adults can be more likely to meet their demands in their community in order to keep the family running as harmoniously as possible.

Children who have had a lot of life-stress and trauma are often more likely to grow Strange.

What is ADHD?

Attention Deficit Hyperactivity Disorder (ADHD) is a mental health condition which can cause hyperactive and impulsive behaviour levels above average. Individuals with ADHD can often find it difficult to concentrate their attention on a particular task or sit still, for a long time.

ADHD can occur in both adults and children. This is a condition accepted by the American Academy of Psychiatrics (APA). Know about forms and signs of ADHD in adults and children alike.

Symptoms of ADHD;

The ADHD is associated with a wide variety of behaviours. Some of the more popular ones include:

- Having difficulty concentrating or concentrating on the activities.
- Forget about accomplishing the tasks.
- Are easy to confuse.
- Having trouble sitting still.
- Interrupting people while speaking.

Whether you or your child has ADHD, any or all of the signs may be present. The symptoms depend on what form of ADHD you have. Explore a list of common child ADHD symptoms.

Types of ADHD.

The APA has divided the disorder into three groups, or forms, to make definitions of ADHD more accurate. Such forms are primarily inattentive, primarily impulse-hyperactivity, and a mixture of both.

Predominantly inattentive.

As the name suggests, people with this form of ADHD find it incredibly difficult to concentrate, complete tasks and obey instructions.

Researchers also agree that many children with the inattentional form of ADHD will not be treated correctly because they don't appear to disrupt the classroom. Between girls with ADHD this form is most popular.

Predominantly hyperactive-impulsive type.

People having this form of ADHD typically display hyperactive and impulsive behaviour. This may involve fidgeting, interrupting people while talking, and being unable to wait for their turn.

While carelessness is less of a problem with this form of ADHD, it can still be challenging for people with primarily hyperactive-impulsive ADHD to concentrate on tasks.

Hyperactive-impulsive type mixed with inattentive type.

This is the most prevalent form of ADHD. Individuals with this form of ADHD combined exhibit both inattentive and hyperactive symptoms. Those involve an inability to pay attention, a propensity to impulsivity and above-normal behaviour and energy levels.

The form of ADHD that you or your child have will decide how he or she is handled. With time the type you have may change, and the care can change too.

ADHD in children.

One in 10 children aged 5 to 17 receive a diagnosis of ADHD, making this one of the most severe childhood neurodevelopmental conditions in the US.

In general, ADHD is associated with school problems for children. Children with ADHD frequently run into trouble in a regulated classroom environment.

Boys are more than twice as as likely to obtain an ADHD diagnosis as girls. That may be because boys appear to exhibit hallmark hyperactivity symptoms. Although some girls with

ADHD may have the stereotypical hyperactivity signs, there are others who do not. Girls with ADHD in certain situations can:

- Daydream sometimes.
- Be more hyper-talkative and not hyperactive.

Most ADHD signs can be normal childhood habits, and it can be difficult to identify what is and what is not linked to ADHD.

Who causes ADHD?

While ADHD is popular, doctors and researchers are still not sure what causes the disorder. It is thought to have roots in neurology. Genetics can play a part, too.

Work indicates dopamine loss is a factor in ADHD. Dopamine is a brain chemical which helps to transfer signals from nerve to nerve. It plays a part in inducing actions and emotional responses.

Other research indicates a variation in brain structures. Findings suggest that individuals with ADHD have less amount of gray matter. Gray matter includes the areas of the brain which help with:

- speech.
- Self-regulation.
- Determination.
- Controlling muscles.

Researchers continue to study possible causes of ADHD, such as smoking during pregnancy. Find out more about the possible causes of ADHD and its risk factors.

ADHD Testing And Diagnosis.

There is no single test that can say whether you have ADHD, or your kids. A recent study demonstrated the advantages of a new method for diagnosing adult ADHD, but many physicians feel it is not feasible to make an ADHD diagnosis based on one method.

The doctor will evaluate any signs you or the child have experienced in the past six months to make a diagnosis.

The doctor is likely to collect input from teachers or family members, and can use checklists and scales for symptoms analysis. They'll also do a physical test to check for any health problems.

If you think you or your child are suffering from ADHD, speak to your doctor about having an assessment. You can also speak to their school counsellor for your kids. Schools assess children periodically for issues that could impact their educational success.

For the evaluation, make information and concerns about you or your child's actions to your doctor or counselor.

If they suspect ADHD, they can refer you to an ADHD specialist, or your kid. It can also recommend scheduling an appointment with a psychiatrist or neurologist depending on the diagnosis.

ADHD Treatment.

Usually treatment for ADHD involves behavioural therapy, medications, or both.

Therapy types include psychotherapy, or talk therapy. You or your child will explore how ADHD impacts your life through talk therapy, and ways to help you handle it.

Another form of therapy is comportemental therapy. The intervention will help you or your child learn how to track and treat their behaviour.

Medication can also be a great benefit when dealing with ADHD. ADHD drugs are formulated to affect chemicals in the brain in a way that helps you to better control your urges and behaviours.

Learn more about recovery options and behavioural therapies which can help relieve the symptoms of ADHD.

Medication For ADHD.

Stimulants and non-stimulants are two primary types of drugs used to treat ADHD.

The most frequently prescribed drugs for ADHD are stimulants of the central nervous system (CNS). These medications function by increasing the dopamine and norepinephrine concentrations of the brain chemicals.

Examples of such medications include stimulants dependent on methylphenidate (Ritalin) and amphetamine (Adderall).

If stimulants are not working well for you or your child or cause alarming side effects, your doctor can recommend a non-stimulant medication. Some non-stimulant medicines function by increasing norepinephrine levels in the brain.

These medicines include atomoxetine (Strattera), as well as other antidepressants such as bupropion (Wellbutrin).

Natural Treatments For ADHD.

As well as-or other than-medicine, it has proposed several treatments to help relieve symptoms of ADHD.

For example, adopting a healthy lifestyle may help control ADHD symptoms for you or your child, the Centers for Disease Control and Prevention (CDC) recommends:

- follow a safe, balanced diet.
- For a total of 60 mins of physical activity a day.
- Win plenty of sleep.

- Limit average screen time from telephones, laptops and televisions.

Research have also shown that yoga, tai chi, and outdoor activities can help relax the overactive minds and relieve the symptoms of ADHD.

Meditation of mindfulness is yet another choice. Research in adults and teenagers has demonstrated beneficial effects of meditation on concentration and thinking patterns, as well as on anxiety and depression.

Potential strategies to help alleviate ADHD symptoms are also to avoid such allergens and food additives.

Any child with ADHD that shows signs of oppositional behaviour needs appropriate care that typically requires a combination of medication as well as family therapy; The first step is to ensure the child's ADHD is regulated. "Seeing that oppositional behaviour is frequently associated with stress," Silver says, "you have to tackle the root of stress— the symptoms of ADHD— before moving to behavioural problems."

Riley says, "If a kid becomes too impulsive or overwhelmed he won't be able to concentrate on the therapies we use to handle oppositional behaviour," he says, "he won't get very far. So the stimulant drugs are something of a blessing for many children with ADHD so oppositional behaviour. Some of the bad behaviour just drops off. "But ADHD treatment is rarely what it takes to control oppositional behaviour. When a child demonstrates only moderate or unusual oppositional behaviour, the trick could well be using do - it-yourself behaviour-modification strategies. Nonetheless, if the oppositional behaviour is serious enough to affect home or school life, it is best to work with a family therapist specialized in childhood behavioural problems.

The doctor will check the child for mood and anxiety disorders. Everyone can trigger oppositional behaviour and everyone calls for their own form of treatment. The therapist can also prescribe cognitive therapy for the boy, to help him cope with tough circumstances effectively.

Why parent instruction may enhance the actions of children with ODD.

Nonetheless, in most situations the therapy of choice for ODD is parent intervention instruction, in which parents are advised by the family therapist to modify the ways they respond to the actions of their child— both good and bad. The parents practice what they've learned in weekly sessions, and report on their success to the therapist.

"Parent preparation is simply about carrots and sticks," Brady says. "At the end of the rope, you are trying to offer encouragement and incentives to your child for their cooperation. They spell out straightforward repercussions for misbehaviour on the stick end, usually including a time-out or the elimination of a reward.

Education in parent management is also highly successful, with the child's actions significantly improving in four out of five situations. Parents who receive the training usually report greater marital satisfaction and better behaviour from their other children.

Although some parents are balking at the idea that they are the ones in need of instruction, "they have to learn how to avoid going with the child into the arena and get down to the level of squabbling," Silver says. Many parents feed the issue by implementing unnecessarily strict or incoherent discipline. Instead, parents must reassert their authority by creating well-defined incentives and punishments, and then systematically and dispassionately enforcing them.

"My most significant concept is that parents do not personally follow Unusual behaviour," Riley says. "Remain calm and polite every time you walk in. Kids in opposition have sensors for adult animosity. If they grab your rage, they'll suit it.

Riley proposes an approach to "two free requests": "Give him two minutes to respond when you ask your child to do something When he does not comply, tell him gently,' I'm asking you to pick up your coat a second time now. Do you understand what I'm asking you to do and if you don't, what are the consequences? Please make a smart decision.' If you have to inquire a third time, the prearranged result will kick in— the television will go off for an hour, or the video game will be taken away.

How Do Parents Handle Positive Behaviours?

It's not a new idea to reward good behaviour or punish poor conduct, but it's easier said than done with oppositional kids. Parents ought to reign in their desire to yell or spank. Around the same time, they need to know how to replace "non-aversive punishments" like time-outs or the loss of privileges.

Most oppositional children's parents are so focused on negative habits that they have avoided reinforcing good ones. But positive reinforcement is the essence and soul of training in parent management.

"Invariably, parents come to therapy with the intention of mitigating, removing or reducing the actions of issues," writes Alan Kazdin, Ph.D., in the therapist's Parent Management Training manual. Yet according to Kazdin, director of the Child Study Center at Yale University in New Haven, Connecticut, parent teaching is now stressing the idea of "positive opposites." "For instance," says Kazdin, "parents are being asked what to do if they want their child to stop crying, slamming the door or throwing things that can be broken. The answers include encouraging gentle conversation, shutting the door softly, and respectfully treating things and not throwing them away. "Kazdin believes that helping parents learn to appreciate good behaviour is one of the greatest challenges faced by therapists. He says parents are often "hesitant about endorsing a behaviour or even using reinforcers because they believe the behaviour does not require any intervention. My child knows how to clean his room, he just refuses to do it,' is a common parental statement.' How parents can give a Defiant Child more meaningful praise.

We will be excited when parents do bid praise. "An unenthusiastic' Excellent' remark is unlikely to alter child behaviour," Kazdin says. Praise should state the praiseworthy action and, preferably, should include a non-verbal gesture. You might say, for example, "the way you played so quietly while I was on the phone was wonderful!"And then kiss your son.

Appropriate rewards and punishments differ between the girls. The more creatively you tailor your curriculum to the unique capacities and needs of your child, the better. Yet as Russell Barkley, Ph.D., professor of psychiatry at Charleston's South Carolina Medical University, writes in Your Defiant Baby, "Creativity is always an advantage to baby-rearing but it can not hold a candle to consistency. Consistency with how you handle your child — how you set laws, express standards, pay attention, promote good behaviour, and enforce repercussions on poor behaviour — is the secret to cleaning up the act of your kid. "Never lose sight of the reality that opponent children generally have a lot to give until their conduct is regulated. "Oppositional children are also pretty fun and bright too," Riley says. "They appear to be positive, and to be very unique, with their own way of looking at the world. When you have worked through their resistance, there's a lot to think about. "Is ADHD a disability?

While ADHD is a neurodevelopmental condition, it is not treated as a learning impairment. And the effects of ADHD will make learning difficult for you. However, in certain individuals who also have learning disabilities, ADHD may occur.

Teachers should chart individual instructions for a student with ADHD to help alleviate any impact on children's learning. This may involve providing additional time for tasks and exams, or creating a program of personal reward.

While this is not necessarily a disorder, ADHD can have consequences that last a lifetime. Learn more about the possible effects that ADHD can have on adults and kids and services that can help.

ADHD And Depression.

If you or your child has ADHD, then depression is more likely to occur as well. In addition, in children with ADHD the incidence of major depression is more than five times higher than in children without ADHD. It was found that up to 31 percent Reliable Source of adults with ADHD do have depression.

It may sound like an unfair double whammy but know that therapies for both conditions are available. Also, the procedures overlap. Talk therapy can be of use in both cases. Sometimes also other antidepressants, such as bupropion, may help ease the symptoms of ADHD.

Getting ADHD does not, of course, mean that you will have depression, but it is important to know that this is a possibility.

Fish Oil Reduces ADHD symptoms.

Dealing with ADHD is a challenge to parents ' best, and a daunting challenge for a child. The effect of time, stress and cost on a family, a school and a community can not be overestimated. The most affected is the boy, because he can not understand his situation. Disorder of attention deficit hyperactivity (ADHD) can devastate a child's life and continue its devastating effects into adulthood. Based on the care given the condition has significant social and health consequences. This threat to people's health as well as society has focused a lot of medical studies on this one disease. As a result, there is a good professional capacity to treat the condition and significantly reduce its effects on those affected. Numerous studies have shown that fish oils can help patients with ADHD, and give them more control over their lives. This essay will describe the effects of ADHD, the widely used treatment regimes and opioid changes, in particular the use of fish oils. These interventions have made the effect of fish oil supplements a major factor in social, cultural, and quality of life.

ADHD is a condition which inhibits concentration and focus even for the slightest mental activity. Children are particularly sensitive to the condition because it influences their learning and development. Inability to concentrate affects learning greatly. Failure to concentrate means confusion is still present, even to adults. Distraction leads to impulsive actions which in effect causes additional problems in a school setting in particular. Hyperactivity may be a factor, as well. The combination of all these traits in one adult complicates the ability of that person to learn and to socialize. When the person ages, symptoms of ADHD that manifest in normal developmental difficulties that come with relationships between adolescence and adults. By addition, ADHD is becoming much more difficult to diagnose and to treat. For all these reasons ADHD has gained significant attention in the psychological community for many years leading to fruitful treatment courses. Treatment regimes are usually a combination of psychotherapy and medication that varies with each patient. Treatment also depends on certain factors which can complicate diagnosis and affect therapy and medication choice.

Common disorders which include learning disabilities, oppositional defiant disorder, and disorder of behaviour alongside ADHD. Disabilities in learning result from poor comprehension or inadequate processing of knowledge that poses barriers to learning by impacting comprehension. A child will misinterpret something, and then add the lesson to the learning process. By undermining learning, the corruption degrades proper education. Many ADHD patients exhibit high intelligence, but their failure to interpret information properly works against the innate intelligence. Teachers who are not qualified to manage such issues can not recognise ADHD as soon as possible or respond well enough to minimize harm and maintain order in classroom.

Oppositional condition of defiance is expressed with stubbornness and defiance even among adults. Patients show strong resistance to authority as it goes against their wishes. This creates disciplinary situations in school and at home which endangers the recipient from attending school or other personal activities. This persistent source of stress impacts work security in adults.

Disorder of behaviour includes acting out, lying, cheating or bullying. The apparent affront to the laws of justice, puts these patients in direct conflict with the laws as well as the law and in contrast to other students or individuals ' best interests. School expulsion is a common solution when school administrators have exhausted all methods for ensuring a balance of the interests of a single student and the rest of the student body. During later life this adverse effect alone has enormous social consequences.

Any of these factors brought into adulthood generate severe relationship problems that impact both family and work life. The inability to learn in combination with erratic, impulsive behaviour and a lack of focus causes accidents and poor performance which makes it difficult to keep a job. Personal relationships suffer as a result of an apparent failure to share accountability. Marriages often fail, and parenting often fails, and probably propagates the problems to another generation. Other severe associated conditions can include depression and other depressive disorders with apparent serious consequences, including the condition of Tourette. Any of these conditions derive from the disorder's stress and emotional insufficiencies. Others, especially the drugs, come from the treatments themselves.

ADHD comes in three main classes: predominantly hyperactive-impulsive, predominantly inattentional, and a combination of the other two. The hyperactive-impulsive type is most disruptive to a student class, or even inside the home. The patient with ADHD becomes the focus of attention which disrupts the required good order in a functional situation. The inattentional class is less dangerous to the structure of society, but more dangerous to the person who does not attract attention to himself and may well be ignored. The combination is most destructive, as the offender multiplies at least twofold of his challenges. Diagnosis of the severity of the condition is a crucial factor in the management of the condition.

The financial, social, and psychological characteristics of the individual involved are vitally important in deciding the specific care received which underlines the requirements that a physician should track the care constantly and consistently. ADHD may be triggered by varying physical, environmental, and social factors in each case. Some treatment regimens contain medications. There are more than 17 licensed medications and treatments currently available in the United States for use in ADHD cases. The intensity and the consequences must be individually considered. Some of the drugs are stimulants, like the common Ritalin. Anti-depressants, particularly in adults, are needed in some cases to lessen the disorder's effects. Needless to say, the use of such medications can cause unpleasant side effects.

Current drugs ' more common side effects include lack of appetite, loss of sleep, and more rarely, tics or repeated movements that unexpectedly occur as sounds or gestures.

More severe side effects include mental deficits and even hallucinations and suicides. ADHD is a question of attitude. In any treatment regime the brain is the center of attention which explains the broad range of symptoms and complications.

Impact of Fish Oil on ADHD.

ADHD was related to a variety of social ills including academic failure, school rejection, truancy and substance abuse, family discord and violence. The advancement of therapies in many of these cases has seen developments in psychotherapy and medication. One of the most important advances in standard treatment regimens has been the use of dietary alternatives or supplements. Fish oil, specifically omega 3 fatty acids, is among the most effective supplements.

Numerous school studies have shown that daily dose of fish oil increases concentration, reduces hyperactivity and enhances learning. One big study in England resulted in a 66 percent decrease in extreme ADHD and impulsive behaviour along with a 72 percent decrease in attention disorders. Test results not only increased but the initiative opened a door for other students to avoid disciplinary expulsions and exclusions. It is a highly important topic in the United Kingdom that has seen an rise in expulsions of 19 per cent in recent years.

For another study, adolescents in another district in the UK showed an increase in 7 percent in test scores of behaviourally disabled pupils after just 12 weeks of fish oils therapy. Improvements were particularly pronounced in the reading tests. The operation had affected girls even more than boys.

Violent activity was significantly decreased in prison population reports. The use of fish oil in Singapore decreased aggressive activity among the prison population by 33%. Such studies suggested that further work is required to ascertain the true causes of the effectiveness and effects of fish oil on treatment regimes and the use of other less natural medicines.

The Fish-Oil Magic.

Fish oil contains two fatty acids, important for the growth of the brain. In short, those two acids ' absence or shortage does not allow the brain to function properly. The regular American diet does not contain adequate amounts of those acids. That may well account for the population's growing incidence of ADHD. Those two omega-3 acids are part of a group of long-chain acids which are distinct from sources other than fish found in the short chain omega-3 acids. In terms of human metabolism the distinction needs to be clarified.

Fatty acids in essential functions of the body are biochemically important to the metabolism and health. The body uses the nutrients in our diet to create the different building blocks that make us who we are. Metabolism requires the reaction of certain substances in certain pathways and the formation of chemical systems which support our body functions. In many of these tasks, the brain is important particularly for the mental components that deal with intellect, emotion and power. The body runs out of materials at some point. That is the ADHD case.

The two acids DHA (duosahexaenoic acid) and EPA (eicosapentaenoic acid) are very essential for proper heart, nervous system, kidney, liver, and brain function. DHA as a constituent of cell membranes in the brain is especially important. In ADHD patients, particularly less than normal brains are the density of the cell membranes and the brain in areas regulating attention. For these essential areas, the long-chain fatty acids DHA and EPA provide the content materials. The simpler and more intuitive method is to supply them directly. Sometime, though, diet shorts the cycle. Short omega-3 acids in non-fish sources may be transformed to DHA and EPA, but this is an additional biochemical step that is statistically inefficient. Supplementation of your diet by direct inclusion of fish in the diet or omega-3 fish oil supplements is much simpler for an person.

Improved fish consumption is nice but it is complicated. Some fish are better DHA and EPA sources than others which can restrict direct dietary approach. Some fish have very few of those acids at all in their oils. New fish are also more vulnerable to heavy metal pollution. Such impurities themselves constitute health hazards and will counteract the beneficial effects of the increased fish oil. Additives provide the best options for sufficient concentrations of fish oil.

Additives are to include refined fish oils. It ensures the oil is extracted from the right fish and the impurities are cleansed. Oil is also enriched with vitamins that would usually be lost by heavy use in case of fish oils and this is another appeal for the oil itself. The manufacturing process allows for a tightly controlled process that produces superior goods in large quantities at lower prices. It provides an economic benefit as compared with traditional ADHD medicines. For short, formulated supplements do without the hazards offer all the benefits of fish oil.

The Benefits of Fish Oil.

Fish oil has contributed benignly in multiple studies to relieve the ADHD symptoms. The alleviation is beneficial in the sense that the regimes for fish oil minimize the requirements for some of the stimulants and antidepressants that cause some powerful side effects. The use of fish oils promotes diagnosis and treatment by simplifying the symptoms which need to be treated. Taken correctly, fish oils reduce severe side effects such as depression, anxiety and suicide while reducing sleep and appetite losses. Good rest and healthy eating keep an patient safe from certain complicated health issues that complicate treatments even more. Medicines get in the way of one another. Consumers should consult a doctor about dosage in specific circumstances, but fish oil supplements do not require prescriptions and doctor supervision. The fish oil is a natural dietary choice that shows promising results in relatively short time. And there are other important benefits like this.

Some of the social problems that arise from ADHD are minimized or removed considerably. Conduct and actions that should have removed children from school and/or sent them to jail was greatly reduced. Such studies confirm several other findings that demonstrate the beneficial effect of fish oil on memory, attention and language abilities.

Research in Sweden have shown that children aged 8-18 who take fish oils had 50 percent less activity with ADHD. These assessments have confirmed the changes in test score and the results seen in many other studies on attention and memory. More and more physicians prescribe fish oils, and see that ADHD is more successful than Ritalin. Some schools recorded the effects of fish oil as raising scores by as much as two grades between students taking fish oil and those not taking fish oil. This performance soothes a huge amount of the tension and anger that comes with the illness for the patient. The increased periods and concentration of attention allows effective performance and focus that not only empirically increases progress but also offers trust that psychologically strengthens that progress. Success increases efficiency. All around, social relations are healthier, and even the adults are more successful.

Medically, the DHA and EPA-containing fish oils are very healthy. The FDA has found that if too much oil is taken or if it is not pure, there are certain side effects. Fish oil slightly thins the blood, and may magnify the effects of any other anticoagulants that an person can take. The oil may also increase the development of bad cholesterol in certain patients and it would be best to consult a doctor about dosage if such conditions are an significant current health factor. However, in general, normal do is healthy, and in a few cases may cause only mild symptoms of gas and incontinence.

All the advantages of fish oil, especially DHA and EPA, come in its simplicity. Second, its root is simplicity. Fish is a regular part of the diets and foods common to people. Fish oil supplements are added value by the fact that processing is simple and purifying. Second, the limited period for efficacy, typically about 12 weeks, as well as its long-term effectiveness and protection suggest fish oil as a significant complement to traditional medicines, if not substitute. Third, fish oil is much less costly than other ADHD drugs, but this is negligible when compared to long-term care rates, which often have to deal with extenuating situations and side effects. Fourth, the implications of recent research and implementations in the world's public structures suggest that fish oil has the potential for significant social impact particularly in areas where action is most important for good order and discipline.

Fish oil may not be the solution for ADHD but it has played an significant part in the condition treatment. By itself, the alleviation of anxiety in the minds of parents dealing with not only the behaviour but the effects of treatment for ADHD is important. This is one of the social advantages of the treatments of fish oil. Health-wise, socially and economically fish oil has an number of well-documented benefits. The minuscule cautions that must be insignificantly applied when using fish oil black.

Strategies for Dealing with a Defiant Child.

It can be incredibly difficult to raise a child with an oppositional defiant disorder, because you feel like everything is a constant fight. You just want to make your child do his homework, clean up his toys, get ready for school, and so on and you're constantly faced with refusal.

I have had several parents and teachers as a behavioural analyst and school counselor asking for guidance about how to approach this kind of rebellious behaviour.

Many also believe that reinforcement for healthy actions is just offering incentives for good behaviour, and when it doesn't work they believe the program isn't working. I have learned repeatedly that reinforcement for good actions doesn't work from people who didn't use it properly. Although a piece of positive behavioural help helps kids win privileges instead of taking them away, it's so much more than just that. It is a way to talk, act, and react to behaviour 1. Set goals in advance and encourage your child to gain opportunities to live up to those goals. To promote obedience, this is much more effective than punishing the child or taking away privileges when they don't do what you want them to do.

Let your child have a say in what they're working for. It places the ball in their court and helps children to obtain privileges. They know what to expect and know what to do to earn the things they enjoy. They always feel a sense of satisfaction in earning what they've worked for.

When your child starts to get off track, remind him what he's working for instead of telling him what you'll take away if he doesn't listen. Evidence indicates that children and teenagers, when they have the ability to receive something, are far more likely to do what is required than when they are told that you will take something from them.

Using transition warnings to let your child know what's next.

Here's an example, "In ten minutes it's time to turn off your video games and come eat dinner" or "It's time for homework after this show." Give some more reminders as the time is running out (e.g., it's time for dinner in two minutes). For children who don't have a sense of time, a timer or visual timer may help.

Act, just don't react.

Should not get upset when you witness your child's stubborn behaviour, and lose your temper. Take a step back then and tell your child you don't approve of the action and she needs to quit. Tell her that you are going to think about the repercussions at a later time where all of you can speak calmly.

This will give your child time to focus on her actions and the potential consequences. You not only use the opportunity to calm down but you also encourage her to do the same.

Strengthen Consequences.

For the most part, successful effects may be divided into two categories: removals and impositions.

A removal is taking away something from the child, like your attention, an exciting environment, or an enjoyable activity. The most commonly used and most well-known elimination is a time out. Some successful removals include banning the child from social activity, removing devices for a specified amount of time, or leaving the park immediately, a friend's home, or a family party when a disrespectful conduct takes place.

Impositions are consequences which impose upon the child a new circumstance. Paying his own money into a fine family pot, doing extra work, running mom's orders because he exploited the luxury of being alone at home by having friends over without permission— these are impositions.

No doubt, it takes time and resources to impose the effects. But if you don't follow through with penalties for poor behaviour, you're going to send out the message "If you wear me down, you'll finally get your way."

Keep Your Power.

When you negotiate with your child in an argument, you reinforce the child's belief that they have the right to defy you, which may lead to even more defiant behaviour.

The next time your child wants to drag you into a fight for control over something, just say, "We've been thinking about this and I've told you what's going to happen. We won't talk about it anymore, "and then we'll leave the room.

You take all the strength with you, as you depart. Know that the more you engage in an argument with your kids, the more power you give up.

Use empathic phrases to demonstrate that your child knows how he / she is feeling.

Imagine how you'd feel if someone walked into your room and said "go off the computer and go to bed." Even though they're children and are supposed to obey the laws of adults, they still have the same emotions that you'd have in that kind of scenario. You can show them that you understand how they feel with a comment like "I know that you're really enjoying your computer time and you don't want to shut it off, but tomorrow you need to get some rest for school. Tomorrow, you will have some time on your machine again.

Phrase instructions in the positive and delete the word "can."

For instance, instead of "stop jumping on the furniture," or "can you stop jumping on the furniture?"In a calm but comfortable tone, try something like" sit down "or" get off the couch. When possible have an alternate activity or redirect them to something they want to do like "let's do jumping jacks together" or "there's some puzzles / blocks to play with." Children react much easier when you tell them "what to do" rather than "what not to do." Anything you want your child to do, you can phrase in the positive by giving them a specific example about what you want them to do. It's also always helpful to offer an example like "you can fall" or "that will harm the sofa."

When your child meets your standards or listens to your orders, use explicit praise.

Such examples include "excellent job picking up your toys," "you've been so focused this evening during homework," "nice job listening to directions," etc. Clear reinforcement or acknowledgment of healthy behaviours reminds the child what habits you try and reinforces them.

No second chances and no negotiation.

When you don't want to perpetuate bad habits, coherence is important. When your kid is mature enough to grasp the effects of behaviours, don't give him repeat chances. It just tells him not to take your own rules to heart.

Do not negotiate for improved conduct or give rewards or benefits in exchange. You encourage your child to test just how far they can drive you.

If when you arrive for a play date your son calls his friend a rude name, say firmly "We're not talking like that. We are going home now so you can spend some time talking about what you've been doing. "Insist he's apologizing and then leave. No ifs, buts, ands.

Do not negotiate for improved conduct or give rewards or benefits in exchange. You only encourage your child to test how far they can drive you before you strike another deal.

Develop on the better.

Check that you draw on your children's positive attitudes and behaviour. Praise your kids for their good attitudes, such as praising them for displaying a cooperative attitude. Positive development will go a long way in raising a healthy child.

Families can see a major decrease in challenging behaviour by making a quick turn toward rewarding good behaviour instead of responding to evil.

Set daily times to converse with your boy.

Sit down with your child in a moment of relaxation when things are going well and you are not expecting an imminent power struggle. Let her know your goal is to keep her healthy and help her grow into a responsible, successful, self-reliant adult who will be as content and fulfilled as possible in life. Remind her that, when growing up, the family has laws and values in place for their future, not to cause her grief.

Pick your wars.

Parenting is exhausting enough when things go well but when one of the kids is intentionally misbehaving, the problems intensify. So pick how you wisely spend your money!

Let's say your high school teacher decides to wear too big pants, because that's the trend. Would you really want to start the day off in a negative way by hassling him about his choices about fashion? In the other hand, if he tells you that he doesn't go to school because he doesn't feel like it, it just won't work. Save your emotional resources to more important things, not to mention your child's.

One of the most important lessons I have learned in my 18 years of parenting is that you can't change the mindset of your child until you first change your own. That takes us to number three of strategy.

If possible give your child choices.

Examples include, "The green or red shirt you want to wear?"Would you first like to do your math or read homework?" Would you like to set the table, or take the garbage out?"

Say what you think, and say what you're doing.

If you tell your child that before he can play outside he has to pick up his toys, make sure that you follow through with your agreement and uphold your end of the deal. Keep away from hollow threats (punishments you'll never be going through). Your child will come to know what your words are worth. When you don't mean what you're doing he / she isn't going to take you seriously.

Use the child's schedule, which builds in chores, homework (if applicable), self-help tasks (shower, brush teeth, etc.) and enjoyable activities if possible. Participate your child in drawing up the timetable. Insert the enjoyable activities into the schedule so that your child alternates between preferred activities and non-preferred ones. Until going on to the next section one part of the plan needs to be complete. Please bear in mind that children with idle time on their hands are searching for things to do, so structuring their time will relieve such impulsive activities such as running / jumping around the house.

Avoid complaining about your child's behaviour, lengthy lectures or sarcastic remarks. Stick to your rules and don't compromise, go back and forth or argue with your kids. If your child continues to protest or tantrum after you have mentioned the rule and shown empathy, let him / her know you will no longer be addressing it. Don't take a temper tantrum to heart. When the tantrum is over you should thank your child for calming down, offer empathy if needed again, and listen if your child needs to speak about his / her feelings. Then steer your child back to his / her planned mission.

When your child is acting dangerous, protect him / her and others from harm, but do not try to compromise with your child or give in to the tantrum to avoid it. In the future, this will only result in more tantrums. If you're ever worried about your child or someone else's health, please call your area's crisis center or emergency number.

Although there is no universal approach that works for every single child, these are the research-backed approaches, and personal experience has proved how well they work.

Ways To Get Your Children To Listen To You And Show Respect For You.

- Set your child's standards and encourage him / her to gain privileges, rather than taking away privileges when he / she doesn't meet your expectations. Tell your child, for example, that he can eat a snack after school every day and then he has to do his homework. He may do an activity of his choice after his homework (e.g. watching TV, playing with toys, going on the internet, etc.). This is much more successful than pushing a child to do his homework, and then saying "That's it. You really don't watch TV!"If he doesn't finish it. If children know the goals ahead of time and have the opportunity to gain something, they are much more cooperative than when they are afraid it will be taken away.

- Encourage your child to become self-employed. Let your child do his / her own best, and only offer assistance if necessary. One technique that I love is waiting for the child to seek support before they give it. On many occasions I watched a child struggle to get the wrapper off his juice box straw. Instead than suggesting "Let me help you here," I'd just wait to see what he'd do. He would ask for support at times, at other times he would finally receive it on his own. The child would get upset in some cases, throw the straw down and say, "I can't do it." This led to a great opportunity to show the child how to ask for support.

- Keep on going. While getting angry is human nature, do your best to maintain a calm tone while implementing your child's laws. You should stick without screaming at what you hear. Enforcing rules without shouting, helps your child to keep calm and still get things done even though you're upset or things don't go your way. It's an excellent example to set for your kids.

- Encourage innovation and encourage it even when you think it's too messy. When your child wants to play in the dirt or do a concoction with a milk-ketchup, let her. You should still sweep the Messes up. When your kid is old enough to clean up their own messes, make sure that she knows in advance that when it's over she'll be asked to clean up. When moving on to an activity of your choosing, make sure that she cleans up. Keep in mind that some kids, particularly younger ones, might need help with cleanup.

- Possible secret abilities to consider. Sometimes kids do things we find irritating which could potentially be channeled into something meaningful. A kid who just wants to run in the house for example could be a strong candidate to be your running partner. A kid who's always knocking on the table at the drums might do well. Ask your child if they want to do something constructive, instead of getting upset and angry about the actions.

- Be consistent and follow through (barring unforeseen circumstances). When you tell your child that he will receive a privilege to complete certain tasks or meet certain requirements, stick to what you have said (e.g., first homework, then television), and make sure you offer the privilege after the task is completed. When you don't let your child earn the rights you gave, he won't take you or your rules to heart. You need to remain solid too. If he pressures you "I'm not going to do my homework!"And try to turn on television, remember in a calm, rational tone,' Homework first, then television.'

- Provide choices for your kids. Children always seek power, since they are often told what to do. Give your child options that you feel confident with (e.g., "Would you like to wear a green shirt or a red shirt?" "Would you like to wear a jelly or butter on your bagel?" "Would you like to do your math or read homework first?").

- If your child shows you what he has done, take an interest. Over the years, working as a school counselor and also among my own peers, I have seen many children showing their parents a image they drew or a dance move they learned, just for the parent to say nothing. Children want to feel like we know about the things they're excited about, the things they have done for the first time, the things they have done on their own, or the things they have made. It's a big deal for them, even though you think it's not a big deal, so that should be enough to making it a big deal for you. Again, that helps with self-esteem and trust.

- Create time for your child to do stuff. Everybody is active. Many days go by so quickly that you appear to have done little on your to-do list, but you have not sat down once. We name life in this craziness, find time. If it's five minutes a day or some weekend hours, spend quality time with your kids. Some examples of a quality time may include talking about your day, going to the park, watching a movie together, going out for dinner, reading a book together, cooking together, fixing something or doing something together, etc. When your child doesn't want to do these things with you, inquire, make an effort, put yourself at your fingertips and try.

- Show your child how good behaviour looks. Children are often disciplined for actions, instead of being shown or shown an alternate method or conduct. Below is a case in point:.

- Teach your kid how to ask for things — if you see your kid steal a toy from another child, try to teach him how to ask for the toy instead of crying or punishing him for snatching it. Tell him how to inquire, and get him to work. Next time you see your child beautifully asking for a gift, remember the action (e.g., when you asked Michael to play with his gift, it was very nice).

- Recognize when your child is putting out a strong effort. People like to know when they have done something right and that includes kids. When people know that they do the right things and impress others they want to do more. Some examples of noticing effort include: "You've really worked hard on cleaning your room; it looks fantastic," "I've seen you studying really hard for that test; you've put a lot of effort into it," "I know you do not like sharing your toys with your brother; but this morning I've seen you sharing very nicely with him! Keep on with the good job!"Even if the affirmation doesn't seem to matter about your child or doesn't seem moved, do it anyway. Their outward reaction can not suit their inner feeling.

- Let your child know that when he / she gets upset about something (teach and show empathy) you understand. Some examples include: "I know you're upset that you weren't invited to that birthday party; it hurts not feeling included." or "I know you're irritated by this homework assignment; let me see if I can help you with it."

- Tell your kid what to do, rather than what not. Study, and my own experience of working with kids for over 19 years, shows that kids (even adolescents) respond better to clear orders than being told not to do something.

Some examples are:

"Go to work on your homework." Instead of "Stop Daydreaming." "Hey, draw on this paper." Instead of "Stop drawing on the walls." "Give me my purse." Instead of "Stop going in my purse." "Walk quietly in the house." Instead of "Stop running in the road.""And" Can you draw from it?"Give the way, and confidently say it.

- 7. Take an interest in telling you all about your child's emotions, feelings, ideas or just his day. Children are also eager to say something to their parents (e.g., "Can you guess what one of my teacher said in class today?" "I think I know what I want to be when I grow up." "If I were president, I'd make sure there weren't bad guys left."). Whether you think it is meaningless, or really don't feel like listening, do it anyway. Once your kids know you're listening and taking note of what they're doing, they're going to come to you about important things, the stuff you want them to tell you. It also helps to make their self-esteem and trust feel as though what they are saying matters. In general, children with a strong self-esteem and self-confidence make better choices.

- 11. 11. Listen to the side of the story that your child has. Taking the time to hear what your child has to say if you receive a phone call from another parent/a teacher about something that your child did wrong. Even if your child was wrong, feeling understood by you is vital to him / her and you may get to know your child a bit better in the process. You may also use the chance as a moment of instruction. For example, if your child kept talking to a friend in class because he was upset about something that happened during recess, speak to your child about possible approaches he / she may have used rather than disturbing the class (e.g., asking to speak to a teacher, talking to his friend at the end of the day, talking to you after school, etc.). This will also be a good time to remind your child that we always have to follow the rules even though we're angry or don't agree with something.

- 12. 12. Tell your kid about you. Although some things are your personal business and not intended for the ears of your child, children feel close to their parents when their parents can open up to them. Tell them about your school days, your interests and your dreams, for starters. If you can open up to him/her your child would be more likely to open up to you.

- Say "good morning," and "good night" (or any variation) and "I love you" every day — we're all busy, but it's an significant one. One among the best things for our self-esteem is feeling cherished, needed, appreciated and acknowledged by our parents. Even if you're not the kind of lovey-dovey, do it for your kids. Take time even for love (hugs, kisses, etc.). Older kids may not want attention, but offering to embrace or even ask for an embrace is a perfect way to show you care.

- Keep in mind: for some children, when you try new techniques, they may actually become more resistant. Before you see progress you can need to be consistent over a period of time. Often, even if you don't get the results you've hoped for, realize that you're doing your part to support your child by constructive strategies. When things sound out of control look for support from a mental health professional or medical professional.

Easy Ways To Enhance Behaviour For Children (Home And School).

Parents and teachers often question themselves how to discipline a child with behavioural issues. Although some kids do have profoundly challenging behaviours irrespective of what approaches we pursue, other kids just need to have adults in their lives make adjustments in how they react, respond, or communicate. This section offers simple techniques you can start implementing to promote positive behaviour in your child / students right now. Both of these approaches are constructive in nature and will help you to interact with your child /student(s) in such a way as to increase their confidence, self-esteem and appreciation for you. Children with good faith and a healthy regard for themselves and the adults show greater cooperation and make positive decisions in their lives.

- Orally, recognize the efforts of children. Clearly tell your kid / student what he / she did you are proud of. For example, you might say "Tonight you have been so focused on your math homework! Keep up the good work," "The way you helped your brother with his math homework was so sweet. "When kids get rewarded for doing the right thing they want to do more. Virtually all kids want adults to satisfy (whether they show it or not) and for most kids, affirmation makes a positive impact. Praise is also an simple way to pay attention to your child, which many children so desperately yearn for.

- Use supportive body language to convey consent to positive behaviour. Positive body language can include a smile, high-five, thumbs up, back slap, and so on. Keep in mind that some kids don't like being handled and would better react to anything like a thumbs up than a pat on the back. Get to see what the kids / students want to see.

- Using the child /student(s) of humor. Make jokes, smile often,listen to their jokes, say something funny, sing anything you would usually say, or something else that would make them smile / laugh (be sure it's age-appropriate).

- Show your kid /student(s) you are happy to see them. Once they come in the house, smile at them; for parents... put your arms out for a hug. Tell about their day, weekend, etc. and listen carefully while they're talking.

- Know that your child / student(s) should be proud of themselves (e.g., "You've been working so hard on the science project, you should be so proud of yourself!"). This helps create internal trust in them so that they can learn to be proud of themselves for being diligent, working hard, being kind to others etc. If they feel successful they are going to succeed.

- Take an interest in the needs of your kid / students. Ask them what they like, get excited about their inventions or successes, ask them about what they want to know, ask them about stuff, etc. Teachers... try to embed the needs of students in the classroom.

- Parents... do things (academic or otherwise) with your children that include something they are involved in, even though it may not be your favorite activity. For other activities let them select topics of interest.

- Recognize feelings of your child / student with empathy. Be patient when they're anxious because they're doing it for the first time, upset because they're having challenging writing assignment, disappointed because they weren't invited to a birthday party, or humiliated because other students laughed about them. Consider saying stuff like "Stop making a big deal about it," "You'll get through it," or "Why do you have such a tough time with this; it's simple." Instead, make empathetic comments like, "I understand this task is stressful for you" or "I understand you're nervous, that's normal when you're trying something new." Also, let them know you're there to support in any way you can.

- Be open minded and do not pass judgement on your kids / students when their opinions, beliefs, feelings or ideas do not suit yours. Of course, expressing your opinion is okay (and dangerous or hurtful conduct is unacceptable), but usually don't have them confused for their opinion. They should/need to feel like they can be transparent in their lives and be with the adults themselves. If kids feel like they are not being punished or wronged, they're more likely to talk to us when there is a real question.

-

- Be a role model of good behaviour. If you want your child to respectfully treat others, you'll do the same. If you want to make your child an honest person, set an honest example for them.

- Respect the promises and laws (barring unforeseen impacts) and stay away from empty threats. If you tell your child / student that after they've done their math assignment they can choose a favorite book to read, make sure you stick to your end of the deal. If you tell your child after his sister has a turn to go on the machine, make sure he has an opportunity to do so. Have clear guidelines that remind your kids that they too have to stick to their end of the deal. If you have a rule like "Homework first, then TV," for example, Follow this rule by making sure that your child completes homework before watching television. Keep away from hollow threats like "If you don't quit I'm going to leave you here" or "I'm going to throw away all of your toys if you don't pick them up." First of all, these comments can be frightening for kids contributing to crying, tannery, etc. and in all probability you won't do such stuff. When you continue to make hollow threats your child will learn that you don't mean what you're saying and therefore learn not to take you seriously. If your kids / students have trust in what you say, and know the limits you've set for them, they will feel a sense of security and confidence that contributes to self-esteem and respect for you. Confident and compassionate children feel good about themselves and the people around them, making them more likely to comply with demands and make healthy choices.

- Using both of these techniques together would most likely result in improvements in positive behaviour over time. While, as a mother, educator, and behaviour professional, there is no perfect solution, I personally find these evidenced-based approaches to be the most powerful in this field over 19 years. Just like a patient who doesn't respond to medical attention right away, we're not giving up. We're always trying.

- If your child is struggling with behaviour dramatically despite having many constructive approaches in place, speak to your child's doctor or the mental health professional to help decide the next steps you should be taking. If you are a teacher with a student with severe behavioural problems (despite many successful strategies), speak to the parent of the child and the school staff (administrator, counselor for advice, etc.).

- Also bear in mind that some kids have great trouble managing their actions or making a different decision because they have not yet mastered alternative / more appropriate strategies to get their point across, or their conduct occurs too quickly (almost impulsively) before they have the opportunity to slow down and think of an alternative. This also happens when the kids feel nervous, scared, sad or frustrated. While this is upsetting for adults, imagine how it feels to the kid who is frequently disciplined, called out, or screamed at because they don't have the ability to copy, talk, or manage to do anything else.

Practical approaches for minimizing childhood impulse behaviours.

Impulsive actions will make your child and the people in his / her life challenging daily situations. Impulsive behaviours are described as acts that occur quickly and seem to occur without noticing or worrying about the consequences. Children diagnosed with ADHD frequently engage in impulsive behaviours, but impulsive behaviours are not necessarily indicative of an adult having ADHD.

Here are some examples of impulse behaviours:

- o Hitting someone or throwing things in angry situations.
- o Jump off a hazardously high surface.
- o papers in class.
- o In the library, playing around.
- o Grabbing stuff from a supermarket shelf.

o   Interrupting / Disrupting someone as they speak or work-Making hurtful remarks before worrying about the consequences.

o   Stealing.

- Create behavioural expectations for future scenarios. What actions would look like, and sound like? Which will become of the activity?

- Of example, if you go to a restaurant, talk about what happens when you get there (e.g. wait to sit down, look at the menu, order your food, etc.) and what the actions of your child will look like (e.g., use an indoor voice, speaking politely when inside the restaurant, waiting appropriately for your meal). Let your child know when you see him / her following the conduct guidelines correctly (e.g. you are waiting very patiently for the food).

- Consult with your child to develop self-awareness about their actions and the ability to solve problems. Help your child get to know his/her impulsive moments, how it affects him / herself and others, and what alternate behaviours he / she may suggest when you and your child have a free time to chat and are both in a good mood.

- Things to think / talk about when discussing your child's self-awareness as it relates to impulsive behaviour:

  - why are you likely to act impulsively?

  - that affecting you?

  - What effect does it have on others?

  - What would you do to make sure you do not make any impulsive decisions while in trouble?

  - What effect do emotions have on impulsiveness?

  - What are some ways of coping with the emotions?

- Evidence shows that children with impulsive behaviours such as those diagnosed with Attention Deficit Hyperactivity Disorder and Oppositional Defiant Disorder display progress when they regularly teach pro-social behaviours such as how to conduct themselves in various circumstances, how to identify problems and propose solutions, and how to recognize and behaviours may be unwelcome in other circumstances

- Let your child reward him / herself with a desired activity or object for going through a particular period of time (e.g. dinner, school, or homework) without any impulsive behaviours (behaviours that interfere with the environment or are harmful / unconsiderate to themselves or others).

- Encourage your child to note if he / she sees / hears impulsive behaviours in his / her environment. Think about what people should have done better. Discuss the situation, and choices.

- Discuss the variations between impulsive behaviours / decisions and non-impulsive ones. Try visualizing what those variations look like by real-life examples. Act out, display photographs or draw various scenarios. Google has a lot of pictures that exemplify impulsive and non-impulsive behaviour. Tell your child to draw a image of someone engaged in impulsive and non-impulsive behaviour, for a fun activity.

- Children with more downtime / unstructured time would be more likely to indulge in impulsive behaviours. Support prepare your child's day so that he knows what to do with himself. Fill it with desired activities (outdoor play, video games, drawing, music) and unfavorable activities (homework, chores, etc.). More time down= less impulsive behaviours.

- Explain to your child that impulsive conduct is often not accepted at work or in the community until you become an adult. Explain real-life repercussions for other forms of impulsive actions (e.g. throwing items into a public location, hitting someone at work, etc.) such as getting shot, kicked out or imprisoned 8. Exercising. Studies show that physical exercise helps to alleviate anxiety, violence and hyperactivity, all of which can put you at risk for impulsive behaviour.

- Know you can't make all impulsive habits go away. Some people may have an impulsive nature sometimes, and while you want to make habits more acceptable, you don't want to discourage someone from being themselves. Everyone can often be a bit impulsive and that can be a positive thing in some cases. Please bear in mind that it should be handled whether it is inconsiderate, hurtful or insensitive to self or others

CONCLUSION

Commonly called Oppositional Defiant Disorder, (ODD). There is a fine line between children who defy authority and who often act poorly and whether such conduct becomes severe enough to be classified as ODD. Each parent is familiar with the "terrible twos" and a certain level of teenage defiance. Whether the behaviour lasts longer (more than six months) or if the defiant behaviour is severe and more frequent than other children of the same age, then we will be able to classify the behavioural problem as an oppositional defiant disorder (ODD).

The young person with Oppositional Defiant Disorder displays a pattern of aggressive, annoying, uncooperative and mean or rude actions towards adults and people who serve authority on a regular basis; The bad behaviour affects the day-to-day life at home, at school, or any other activity the involves the child.

If you consider Oppositional Defiant Disorder in a boy, you also experience other behavioural issues. Depression, anxiety, mood swings, hyperactivity and attention issues are some of the other behavioural problems these Weird kids may encounter.

ODD signs are easy to see. Whether or not they are really Unusual is decided by this form of activity's age and frequency and intensity, as well as the obvious intent, because you know the child (or teen) knows right from wrong, or the correct conduct for the circumstance. Unless the conduct persists consistently despite discipline and stern talks and explanations, and seems to be "on purpose," you may develop Oppositional Defiant Disorder. Bear in mind that at the moment or for a variety of other causes, a time or two of such events can be due to age or irritability, but it is the ongoing unacceptable behaviour that we have to look out for.

Some of the displayed forms of actions in the ODD child or teen are arguing with adults, purposely attempting to annoy or upset another child or adult, despiteful, seeking revenge, saying hurtful things to others, throwing constant tantrums, yelling obscenities or cursing, often accusing others and complaining and refusing to go along with the rules.

We all wonder what in one child and not in another, and sometimes even from the same family, may be the source of such bad conduct! The utter trigger for sure isn't really understood. There seem to be various causes: biological) brain damage, chemical imbalances, hereditary (herited propensity for emotional issues such as depression) and environmental (discipline, care (lack of), and other issues that may be due to parenting or lack of parenting. The exact cause can sometimes never be determined or a variety of causes will occur.

If Oppositional Defiant Disorder is the possible issue for the inacceptable behaviour of your child or adolescent, the place to start would be a comprehensive evaluation by your physician. He'll help identify the problem and help find a remedy or cure for it. He must continue his assessment with a comprehensive medical history and physical examination to make sure there is no physical cause. Only then will child psychologists or other counseling methods be taken after the doctor or medical adviser's advice. You should, however, educate yourself too. There are now plenty of strong sources explaining the treatments for depression and parenting management.